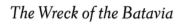

The Wreck of the Batavia

Other books by Simon Leys

The Life and Work of Su Rensham, Rebel, Painter and Madman (Prix Stanislas-Julien, Institut de France)

The Chairman's New Clothes: Mao and the Cultural Revolution

Chinese Shadows

Broken Images

The Burning Forest

The Analects of Confucius (translation and commentary)

The Angel and the Octopus

The Death of Napoleon (Christina Stead Prize for Fiction, Sydney; *The Independent* Best Foreign Fiction Award, London)

Illustrations: *The Two Acrobats* (text by Jeanne Ryckmans)

The Wreck of the
BATAVIA

SIMON LEYS

THUNDER'S MOUTH PRESS
NEW YORK

for Hanfang

THE WRECK OF THE BATAVIA

Published by
Thunder's Mouth Press
An Imprint of Avalon Publishing Group Inc.
245 West 17th St., 11th Floor
New York, NY 10011

AVALON
publishing group incorporated

Originally published by Black Inc., an imprint of
Schwartz Publishing Pty Ltd.
First Thunder's Mouth Press edition January 2006

Internal images: Replica of *Batavia* © 2005, Jaap Roskam,
www.bataviaphotos.com; Torrentius, *Still Life with a
Bridle* © Rijksmuseum, Amsterdam; postcard of *Etel*
courtesy the author; watercolor of the *Batavia* by Ross
Shardlow, courtesy Batavia Yard, Lelystad, Netherlands:
www.bataviawerf.nl.

Library of Congress Cataloging-in-Publication Data is
available.

ISBN: 1-56025-821-7
ISBN 13: 978-1-56025-821-6

9 8 7 6 5 4 3 2 1

Book design by Thomas Deverall
Printed in the United States of America
Distributed by Publishers Group West

Contents

THE WRECK OF THE BATAVIA

The only thing necessary for the triumph of evil is for good men to do nothing.

—EDMUND BURKE

'The book that was not' [†]

FOREWORD

Have you ever had a wonderful idea for a book? There's no need to rush to get started on it, for you can be sure that sooner or later, someone else will have the same idea, and make perfect use of it.

I speak from experience. It is now eighteen years since I first began to dream of telling the story of the wreck of the *Batavia*. I collected nearly everything that was published on the subject; then I went to stay on the Houtman Abrolhos where the disaster took place.

[†] This phrase was borrowed from Victor Segalen, who used it at the beginning of *René Leys*: 'I shall not know anything more about it; I will not insist, I take my leave, going out, respectfully stepping backwards [...] It is with such a confession – ridiculous or diplomatic – that I must end these notes which I have wished to turn into a book. The book shall not be. (By the way, what a beautiful posthumous title for a non-existent book: *The Book that was Not*.)'

For years, I kept pondering the project and jotting notes, but never actually settled down to write the first page of a book which, amid the increasingly derisive scepticism of my family, began to take on a mythical aspect. From time to time, I learned that some new book had just been published on my topic – invariably sending me into a cold sweat – and each time, I would rush to get a copy of it. But no – it was always a false alarm; I saw quickly, with relief, that the author had again missed the target, and this only reinforced my false sense of security. Once or twice, though, I felt the whirr of a bullet, but disregarded the warning.

Then came Mike Dash. With his *Batavia's Graveyard*, published in 2002, this author hit the bull's eye and left me nothing more to say. Dash managed to disentangle the various threads of the complex tragedy and to set personalities and events in their historical context. Above all, he did amazing detective work in the Dutch archives. After carefully reading his detailed study, I put away for good all the documents and notes, sketches and photographs I had gathered over the years; I had no further use for them. In publishing the following pages, my only wish is that they may lead you to Dash's work.

S.L.

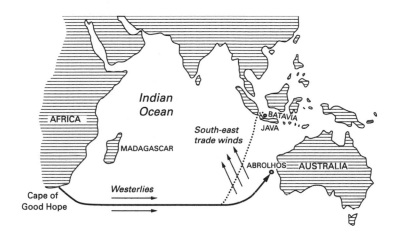

Outline of the Course of VOC Ships Across the Indian Ocean

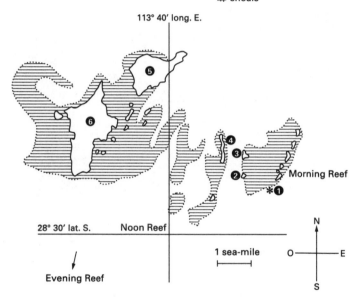

Key to Symbols

1. Location of the shipwreck
2. Traitors Island
3. *Batavia*'s Graveyard
   (Beacon Island)
4. Seals Island
5. High Island (East Wallabi)
6. Wiebbe Hayes Island
   (West Wallabi)

◇ emerged land
≋ shoals

113° 40′ long. E.

⑤

⑥

④
③
②
*❶

Morning Reef

28° 30′ lat. S.   Noon Reef

↓
Evening Reef

1 sea-mile

N
O————E
S

Houtman Abrolhos Archipelago (Northern Group)

Watercolor of the *Batavia* by Ross Shardlow.

Replica of the *Batavia*, Sydney, October 2000, Jaap Roskam.

Torrentius (1589–1644) *Still Life with a Bridle* (Allegory of Temperance). Rijksmuseum, Amsterdam.

θάλασσα κλύζει πάντα
τάνθρωπων κακά[†]

F or three hundred years – from the end of the
fifteenth century to the end of the eighteenth –
Western navigators explored the world and developed
vast commercial empires. Astonishingly, they achieved
these feats with only crude and primitive navigation
technology: today, any sailor going to sea with such
scanty information would be terrified – and rightly so.
They skirted unknown and dangerous shores without
charts or local knowledge, they crossed oceans while
virtually blind. They could never be entirely sure of
their position for one factor was always missing: the
ability to ascertain longitude. Latitude was easy to calculate (when the sun and the horizon are visible, one

---

[†] 'The sea washes away the evils of men'

1

can determine this readily), but navigators wanting to establish longitude had to rely on dangerously vague estimates. This ignorance was finally dispelled when the English invented the marine chronometer, but this basic instrument only came into common use at the end of the eighteenth century.[†]

Throughout its two hundred years' existence, the Dutch East India Company (Verenigde Oostindische Compagnie, abridged as 'VOC'), a true state within a state with its colonies, governors, diplomats, magistrates and army, was the most powerful commercial entity in the world. The company's prosperity was built on the spices which its fleet brought back from the East Indies. The ships of the VOC were heavy, strong three-masted vessels with double oaken hulls, which the Dutch shipyards built continuously, with a speed that could barely meet the relentless demands of the market (the *Batavia*, a giant in her time, was completed in a mere six months). Despite their strength, these ships had a limited life-span: even those that escaped the hazards of sea could seldom survive the strain of more than half a dozen voyages to the East and back. The passage to Java – fifteen thousand sea-miles, more than

---

[†]   On this topic, one must read the fascinating book by Dava Sobel: *Longitude*, Walker & Co, New York, 1995.

two thirds of the world's circumference – lasted about
eight months without any major mishap. Slow and
sluggish with their round bellies, the massive ships
straggled along at an average speed of two and a half
knots (4.5 kms per hour). They hardly answered to the
helm and could not change tack without help from
the sails.

Under sail, the fastest route is seldom the shortest,
as one must above all avoid zones of calm and seek
areas where the winds are favourable and steady. As
time was money on the Western spice market, the
VOC ordered its skippers to follow a specific course per-
fected by experience, one that included some detours.
After the Cape of Good Hope (the only scheduled
port of call for water and fresh supplies), instead of
sailing to the north of Madagascar and then steering a
direct course towards Java, the ships first went south,
near the edge of the Southern Ocean, in order to take
advantage of the powerful westerlies that blow around
the globe from the fortieth parallel down – 'the roar-
ing forties'. Pushed by wind and current, they then
swiftly went east till they thought they had reached
the longitude of the Sunda Straits. From that hypothetical spot, in the middle of an empty ocean with
nothing to confirm their exact position, they changed

course and, broad-reaching under the south-easterly
trade winds, steered north towards Java, still 2000 miles
away.

If they changed course too late – and errors in dead
reckoning were frequent, for due to strong winds and
currents the ships often covered a much greater distance than their apparently mediocre speed led one to
believe – the consequences could be fatal: they would
have to face one of the most inhospitable coasts in the
world, that of Western Australia, where a continuous
wall of cliffs abuts the Indian Ocean for hundreds of
miles without any break or natural shelter. Carried by
a fresh breeze, any ship that approaches this coast at
night runs the risk of being driven ashore; and especially so in the case of the heavy square-riggers that
were unable to change tack swiftly. For these reasons,
the VOC issued strict safety instructions to all its skippers: 'Terra Australis Incognita' was to be avoided at all
costs.

The Dutch, who were the first European navigators
to discover this forbidding coast, never tried to get to
know it, having made the hasty assessment that nothing was to be gained. Not only were the approaches
dangerous, but the resources were nil; one could not
even safely find water. The natives were few, backward

4

and miserable; no trading post could ever hope to prosper there.

Yet, so long as the navigators were unable to calculate their longitude, they ran the risk of inadvertently encountering the Australian continent. In two hundred years, of all the ships that sailed to the East Indies, one in fifty never reached her destination. On the return voyage, one in twenty never saw Holland again. Most of the lost ships disappeared without a trace; one suspects that many foundered on the Australian coast, although the exact number cannot be known. Only a few of these shipwrecks have been accurately identified, sometimes hundreds of years later.

For instance, mystery long surrounded the fate of the *Zuytdorp*. She had left the Cape of Good Hope in 1712, bound for Batavia, and then vanished until, two centuries later, in 1927, an Australian stockman found on a clifftop various objects worn by age and eaten up by rust, but still clearly identifiable: they had belonged to the crew of the lost ship. Some time afterwards, divers discovered what remained of the wreck in the reefs below. It was clear that a group of castaways had managed to climb the cliff and survived for quite a while in this barren spot. Were they perhaps adopted by local Aborigines? One of these tribes shows genetic

5

features that can only be explained, it is said, by contact with Dutch blood.

However, not all the shipwrecks were forgotten. In fact, the earliest, that of the *Batavia*, which occurred in 1629 on the reefs of the Houtman Abrolhos, a group of tiny coral islands some fifty nautical miles off the Australian mainland, was the most famous and also the most fully documented. The three hundred survivors who found shelter on the islands fell under the control of one of them, a psychopath who instituted a reign of terror. This criminal, assisted by a few acolytes whom he had managed to seduce and indoctrinate, led a methodical massacre of the castaways, sparing neither women nor children. Three months later, with two hundred already slaughtered, the bizarre butchery was brought to an end by the arrival of a rescue ship from Java. The leader and his main accomplices were put to death on the spot after being duly examined, tortured and sentenced according to the legal requirements of Dutch criminal justice. The minutes of the trial and the witnesses' statements were carefully recorded; these documents were supplemented by the internal reports of the VOC and the memoirs written soon after the events by two of the principal survivors. A book drawing together most of this information was published less than ten years later. It immediately became a best-seller and was reprinted (and pirated) several times; part of it was eventually translated into French.[†]

It can be said without exaggeration that, in its time, the tragedy of the *Batavia* had a greater impact on the public imagination than did the wreck of the *Titanic* in the 20th century. The comparison comes naturally to mind since in both cases disaster struck, on her maiden voyage, a ship that embodied the pride and the power of her age.[‡]

As centuries passed, the memory of this dark episode faded into oblivion until 1963, when, guided by the remarkable deductions of a local historian, a diver found the wreck.[*]

After the discovery, thorough underwater explorations were conducted. Parts of the ship's structure were

---

[†] Jan Jansz: *Ongeluckige Voyagie van't Schip Batavia* (based on the diary of F. Pelsaert, with the addition of the memoirs of G. Bastiaensz), Amsterdam 1647, 1653, 1665, and M. Thévenet: *Relations de divers voyages curieux*, vol. I, Paris, 1663.

[‡] In proportion, the *Batavia*'s disaster ended with more victims, but paradoxically, many fewer died in the actual shipwreck. On the *Titanic*, passengers committed crimes to save their lives, whereas the slaughter of the *Batavia*'s survivors was senseless – which makes it all the more terrifying.

[*] The fisherman who was my host when I stayed in the islands told me that the location of the wreck had been well known to

retrieved (actually the entire stern, from the keel to the upper deck), as well as some of her cargo, including the ready-hewn sandstones of an ornamental gate intended for the citadel of Batavia. These two majestic structures – the reconstructed stern of the ship and the re-assembled stone portal – now occupy the main hall of the Maritime Museum in Fremantle in Western Australia, where one can also see the rich – and gruesome – results of the archaeological excavations that are still conducted in the islands: countless artefacts, implements, weapons, potsherds; and also bones, skulls and entire skeletons of various victims of the massacres. Once again the *Batavia* became a topic of interest and the subject of many publications: articles, learned monographs, historical novels, popular works, documentary films, even an opera. Finally came Mike Dash's book, which outshines all its predecessors and from which I have drawn much of the information presented here. It offers what will almost certainly remain the most reliable survey of all that can be known on this subject. Of course, one may fear that novelists

---

local fishermen since the fifties, but nobody in this small and tightly knit community had talked to anyone outside about it, fearing the disturbance and sudden influx of visitors that this revelation would inevitably bring.

8

and script-writers will continue to find inspiration in a drama of which all the constituent parts – exotic setting, adventure, shipwreck, violence, sex, horror, suspense and rescue at the last moment – seem to have been devised with Hollywood in mind. But I dare say that their efforts will fail: in such a story, no imagination can compete with the bare facts.

Obviously, without the intervention of a criminal of superior gifts, the aberrant atrocities that followed the wreck of the *Batavia* could never have taken place. This was the decisive factor, and it could not have been foreseen. Yet there was another factor which also played an essential part, one connected to the institutional structure of the VOC: the fact that authority was not placed in the hands of a seaman but rather entrusted to a landsman, the supercargo (*opperkoopman*). This high official possessed administrative, political and commercial qualifications, but all the responsibilities concerning the actual handling of the ship – navigation, seamanship, crew discipline – fell to his subordinate, the skipper (*schipper*), himself seconded by the first helmsman (*oppersteuurman*) and his two assistants. The skipper was therefore not a 'captain' in the modern sense of the word; he was simply an experienced seaman (the VOC would not have entrusted one of its valuable vessels to an apprentice!). Apart from this, he had little, if any, education – the primitive astronomical navigation of the time did not require much theoretical knowledge. But the key point is that, on board, he was not 'master after God', but only master after the supercargo.

The ship, therefore, was under a sort of lame double command. The supercargo gave orders to the skipper, but his orders lacked the authority that only a seaman could muster. The situation produced uncertainty and conflict. On the *Batavia*, this was aggravated by an acute animosity between the two men, who – to make matters worse – had clashed previously in different circumstances, well before this voyage.

The *Batavia*'s supercargo was Francisco Pelsaert, a 33-year-old native of Antwerp. His official title was *Commandeur*, for in principle he was also in charge of five other ships that were supposed to sail in company, though the convoy broke up after calling at the Cape. A gifted and well-educated man, Pelsaert had served with distinction as the VOC representative at the Court of the Great Moghul in Agra. But his health was frail; in India, he had caught a recurrent fever which still incapacitated him for weeks at a time – in fact, it would eventually kill him two years after the shipwreck.

The skipper, Ariaen Jacobsz, was over forty, and therefore one of the oldest men on board (in the seventeenth century, seamen did not live long). A robust and skilful sailor, but a poor navigator, he was wild and coarse, a drunkard and a lecher, bursting with health and brute strength. Ten years earlier, while calling in at India, he had met Pelsaert and quarrelled with him during a drunken binge. This had brought a public reprimand from his superiors, and as a consequence he bore a grudge against Pelsaert, whom he held responsible for his humiliation. In accepting his new post on the *Batavia*, he thus found himself under the command of someone he hated.

While huge for her time, the *Batavia*, with a length of 165 feet (50 metres), was not even twice as long as a modern 'maxi-yacht'.[†] Yet for eight whole months, except for one interruption about halfway for a short call ashore at the Cape, she carried some three hundred and thirty people crowded together in unimaginably

---

[†] But her height is still impressive. The modern replica of the *Batavia*, a masterpiece of naval architecture built in Holland with the same dimensions and same materials, called at Sydney in 2000. In order to reach the inner harbour where large container-carriers and other cargo-boats are berthed, she had to wait for an exceptionally low tide to clear the Sydney Harbour Bridge, which her masthead nearly touched.

close quarters. This teeming population was traditionally divided into two unequal groups: the occupants of the aft castle and the rabble of the foc'sle. In the aft was the great cabin, shared by the staff and some distinguished passengers – a handful of individuals. In the foc'sle was the steerage, which was filled with sailors, gunners and soldiers.

Besides the supercargo, the skipper and the helmsman, the aristocracy aft included an assistant supercargo (*onderkoopman*), Jeronimus Cornelisz, a man about thirty years old who had only recently signed on with the VOC. He was well-educated; he had been an apothecary but various setbacks had brought him to the verge of bankruptcy. However, in boarding ship for the East, he was not fleeing his creditors but the arm of the law. He was closely linked to a scandalous character, the painter Torrentius (1589–1644)[†], who had just been arrested, tortured and condemned for immorality, Satanism and heresy. The authorities were searching for any of his associates.

Among the passengers was a churchman, a Calvinist *predikant*, Gijsbert Bastiaensz, a decent fellow, pious but not very bright, who was travelling with his family

---

[†]   His true name was Johannes van der Beeck. Torrentius is the Latinised form of his name – literally, Brook.

– his wife, seven children and a maid – in the hope of finding a parish in the colonies that could feed him and his numerous tribe. There was also a young woman of the Amsterdam upper class, Lucretia van der Mijlen. It seems that, on a sudden impulse, she had decided to join her husband who was working in a VOC trading post in the East Indies. It was uncommon for Dutch wives of her social milieu to share their husbands' lives in the insalubrious climes of the East, but Lucretia was an orphan; furthermore, her three young children had died in quick succession and her loneliness hung heavily upon her. Her beauty – attested to by several witnesses – would have a disastrous effect on the men around her in the great cabin. She had a young maid, Zwaantie, who had been hastily recruited at the last moment; she was a slut, and would bring her mistress plenty of trouble.

For'ard of the main mast, in the squalid quarters of the sailors and soldiers, were about fifteen women. Most of them had been smuggled on board by their companions and some were suckling babies; two more were later born at sea. The hundred and eighty topmen lived in the upper steerage, kept apart from the soldiers because the two groups did not get on. The soldiers were confined in the lower steerage, a kind of vast

13

pigsty, dark and stifling, so low that one could not stand upright. The soldiers – mostly German mercenaries but also including some Frenchmen[†] – had been recruited by the VOC to reinforce its garrisons in Java. They were officered by two adjutants, old professionals, and a dozen cadets, very young and penniless Dutch aristocrats. There were also gunners, for the *Batavia* carried a battery to see off pirates, natives and foreign competitors. And finally, there was the group of special-ised craftsmen, nicknamed 'idlers' by the sailors because they worked only by day and did not stand watches: the carpenters and sailmakers, the cook and his helpers, and also, of course, the barber-surgeon, the *Comman-deur*'s secretary and the book-keeper.

Even in the best conditions, life at sea (at least till the nineteenth century) was considered by landsmen to be a dreadful ordeal – and rightly so. Though he belonged to a great maritime nation, Samuel Johnson famously summed up this view: 'No man will be a sailor who has contrivance enough to get himself into a jail; for being in a ship is being in a jail with the

---

[†]   Two hundred and fifty years later, Arthur Rimbaud was to enlist in that same colonial army, though it no longer belonged to the VOC; it was now in the service of the King of Hol-land.

14

chance of being drowned ... A man in a jail has more room, better food, and commonly better company.'

And indeed it was a life of unthinkable brutality. The list of its horrors is endless: the stench; the lack of comfort and hygiene (on the *Batavia*, more than three hundred people shared four latrines, two of them in open air swept by spray; only the elite of the great cabin used a chamberpot service); the promiscuity; the lack of fresh air and space; the perpetual dampness; the heat; the cold; the rats; the vermin; the dirt (to save fresh water the sailors sometimes had to wash their clothes in urine); the tainted food, mouldy or full of grubs; the foul water; the coarseness of shipmates; the sadistic discipline; the dreadful and permanent menace of scurvy that swelled and rotted its victims' flesh, turning them into living corpses before killing them off (on ships bound for the Indies, scurvy carried off an average of twenty or thirty men each voyage†).

---

† After seven months at sea, the *Batavia* had already lost ten men to this disease. Scurvy was terrifying because nobody knew its cause – which was in fact a lack of raw vegetables and fruit. The remedy was quite simple, but it was identified, and began to be applied, only at the end of the eighteenth century. The great English navigators, especially Cook and Bligh, at last gave their crews complete immunity by compelling them to drink lime-juice and eat sauerkraut.

The voyage of the *Batavia* started badly. Leaving the Texel roadstead at the end of October 1628, on the second day and not yet out of Dutch waters, she met a violent squall which caused her to run aground on the dangerous Walcheren sandbanks. The skipper eventually managed to float her off with the help of the tide. Fortunately the powerful hull did not suffer any damage, but the ship had nearly been lost. After that, the long journey to the Cape – six months at sea – was without further mishap but tensions had arisen in the great cabin.

The supercargo, Pelsaert, was an irrepressible womaniser. Several times already this compulsion had nearly ruined his career. Once, at the Court of Agra, he had even seduced the consort of a prince; the affair had taken a dangerous turn and almost cost him his life. As for the skipper, Jacobsz, his appetites were no less keen, though he expressed them in a grosser manner. The two soon started to compete for Lucretia's favours, but she resisted their advances. Pelsaert, who was a gentleman, accepted this with good grace. Jacobsz took it badly: to avenge himself against the mistress, he seduced her maid. Zwaantie was immediately more welcoming – she had willingly accommodated a good number already – and took advantage of this new intimacy with the skipper to flout Lucretia and defy her orders. Meanwhile, unbeknown to all, the former apothecary, Cornelisz, also had designs on Lucretia, but because of his rather lowly position was careful to hide his growing obsession.

One can only guess at how unbearably tense and poisonous the atmosphere in the great cabin must have become. These ill-assorted individuals, with their pent-up hatreds, ill-suppressed desires and exacerbated frustrations, were bundled up in the heavy black suits that the Dutch sense of propriety dictated they wear, even in the tropics. Round the common table, three times a day for the hundred and eighty days it took to reach the Cape, they could only glare at each other, stiff, red-faced and oozing sweat.

To some extent, the brief respite offered by the Cape should have relieved the tension. In fact, it prompted the first outburst. To please Zwaantie, the skipper borrowed a jolly-boat and, together with the former apothecary with whom he had become very friendly, went rowing to show off his conquest to the other ships anchored in Table Bay. By the end of this jaunt, Jacobsz was thoroughly drunk and he got into a brawl with some other sailors. Infuriated by this scandal, which besmirched the *Batavia* in the eyes of the fleet, Pelsaert gave him a fierce tongue-lashing. Jacobsz had to bear it with clenched teeth – and swore to avenge himself.

The *Batavia* sailed on, starting the second and last leg of her voyage. With a persuasive eloquence that matched his deviousness, the former apothecary contrived to blow on the embers of the skipper's rage. At the table where they all sat, the hosts of the great cabin had listened on many occasions to the bizarre theories Cornelisz had learned from Torrentius. In fact, they enjoyed them as if they were some sort of clever intellectual game, an original way to while away their long idle hours. For who could honestly believe that Hell does not exist, or that crimes committed by God's elect are not crimes at all?

Cornelisz's private conversations with Jacobsz had taken a more practical turn. The skipper was not one for philosophico-theological speculation, and instead Cornelisz planted in Jacobsz's head the idea – quite feasible – of taking over the *Batavia*. They simply had to get rid of Pelsaert and then Jacobsz would be sole master of the ship. With the help of a few trusted and resolute men, it wouldn't be difficult to control a disorganised and wavering crowd. The ship was carrying huge treasures: twelve chests filled to the brim with silver ingots and coins as well as pearls and other jewels – the mutineers would be wealthy for the rest of their lives. Instead of sailing for Java, they simply had to divert the ship to any settlement of a foreign competitor: the English or the Portuguese would be only too happy to welcome them. Jacobsz, taking advantage of his influence on the sailors, and Cornelisz, relying on the skills that enabled him to insinuate himself everywhere, started to recruit a dozen accomplices. This small group, which reached into the diverse social strata of the ship, was later to form the core of Cornelisz's followers.

A short time after leaving the Cape, Pelsaert suffered another bout of fever that laid him low for a month and almost killed him. Unexpectedly he recovered, but as soon as he was back on his feet the conspirators attempted to set a snare for him. Their plan was to devise a provocation so outrageous that Pelsaert, when confronted by it, would be compelled to impose such harsh punishments that these, in turn, would provoke widespread discontent among the crew. To this end, they decided to make Lucretia their target. The choice of victim was probably due partly to the spite of the skipper and to Zwaantie's resentment, though it may well have also reflected the former apothecary's bizarre and perverse obsessions.

On the empty deck one night, eight masked men from among the mutinous conspirators attacked Lucretia. They pinioned her against the planking, tucked up her dress and petticoat, and smeared her obscenely with tar and excrement. They carried out their plan quickly and vanished into the night. The heinous crime was soon known all over the ship. Pelsaert, who had barely recovered from his illness, was mad with rage and led a sharp inquest. Yet, to the disappointment of the conspirators, he did not take instant reprisals nor enforce extraordinary measures of discipline, and the routine of the ship continued unchanged. In fact, it seems that Lucretia had recognised one of her aggressors, a man close to the skipper. This information, which she must have imparted to the *Commandeur*, gave him food for thought: if Jacobsz himself was behind the foul deed, the whole affair was even more disquieting. The wisest course would be to proceed with great caution and wait until the arrival in Java. Once there, in more secure conditions, he would resume investigations.

But during this uneasy lull, disaster struck.

On the night of the 3rd of June, 1629, the *Batavia*, carried by a fresh breeze, was running under full sails. The moon was bright, and on the second watch of the night, the look-out man thought he saw a white patch on the water straight ahead, as if the sea were breaking over shallows. He warned the skipper, who was on the quarter-deck, but the skipper, believing that it was a mere reflection of the moon, did not change course. He felt perfectly safe: on the day before, his latest reckoning had put the ship 600 miles from the nearest land! In actual fact, he was only forty-odd miles from the Australian mainland and right in the middle of a large group of reefs and coral islets, the Abrolhos group, which a Dutch navigator, Houtman, had discovered by accident ten years before. An instant later there was a tremendous shock, immediately followed by dreadful creaking. Due to her immense weight and the impetus of her speed, the *Batavia* had just 'impaled herself'[†] on a coral ridge.

The usual manoeuvres were rapidly attempted: an anchor was carried by the longboat and dropped in deep water. To unballast the ship, the guns were pushed overboard, and even the main mast was hacked down and thrown into the sea – a needless and desperate sacrifice.

Nothing was of any use. After several hours of frantic activity, it became clear that the ship would

---

†   In Mike Dash's accurate description.

never be floated off; she was now as rigid and motionless as the reef that had broken her course, and she would not budge until the sea, which kept pounding her with blows, eventually broke her to pieces.

Until recently, ships plying the high seas didn't carry efficient life-saving equipment. The lack of this was even more marked in the seventeenth century. The *Batavia*, for instance, had only a longboat and a small yawl, which between them could barely carry fifty men – less than one-sixth of the ship's complement. In any case, these two boats were not designed for life-saving; they served as tenders for transportation, hauling, reconnoitring, communication with the shore and other tasks to do with manoeuvring the ship. When a ship was lost, everything was lost and sailors, however bold and experienced, could not conceive of a time after the shipwreck for which special equipment would be needed.[†] The inflexible discipline that had regu-

---

† More than fifty years ago, when Dr Alain Bombard launched his famous experiments of survival at sea (one remembers that he crossed the Atlantic alone in a small life-raft), his primary objective was to challenge this view prevalent among seamen. He relates the case of a fisherman who, after the wreck of his trawler, found himself adrift in a life-boat in sight of the coast of Brittany: he died within a few hours, with no reason whatever – of simple despair. (See also p. 86–87, below.)

lated all aspects of the life and activity of the crew melted at once in the face of the wreck, as if all authority had inevitably to disappear with the ship itself.

When it became obvious that the *Batavia* was irretrievably lost, chaos reigned. Mercenaries and sailors broke into the stores of wine and spirits and engaged in a wild orgy. Every taboo was swept away: drunken sailors invaded the hallowed quarter deck, forced their way into the great cabin, broke into the chests, took the plumed hats, brocades and golden chains of their leaders, and improvised a frenzied, grotesque and desperate carnival.

By that time dawn had come. By the light of day it became clear that, in her very misfortune, the *Batavia* had been exceptionally lucky. In the west, the way she had come, heavy swell was breaking on the other end of the reef. If the *Batavia* had struck there, the sea would have battered her to pieces in a few hours and, so far from land, nobody would have had the remotest chance of survival. Her current position, however, placed her near a large area of shallows where, at low tide, one could wade towards two islets, one very small, one somewhat bigger. Furthermore, behind these, here and there, long lines of white surf were breaking on low-lying lands. Pelsaert, the skipper and the helmsman had kept the longboat and the yawl under their control. Taking the small islet as their centre of operations, they organised a shuttle service with the two boats to carry most of the shipwrecked to the larger islet, soon named 'Batavia's Graveyard' (*Batavia's Kerkhof*; on today's charts, it is called Beacon Island).

The Graveyard is a triangular piece of grey, arid land. Its soil is made of crushed coral, in which grow dry, low bushes which gusty winds force to the ground. This island is about a quarter of a mile in length, somewhat more than half that in width; one can walk around it in five minutes. To leeward, facing the calmer water of the lagoon, there is a tiny beach of white sand, sheltered enough to provide a good landing place for small boats. In five or six trips, the longboat and the yawl brought more than a hundred and eighty people there, plus provisions and a small quantity of water. More than seventy men, mostly sailors and soldiers bent on staying drunk, remained on the ship, the powerful frame of which had so far resisted the onslaught of the sea. Among them were also a few people whose fear of the water confined them to the false security of the wreck.

Over the next two days, the *Commandeur* organised a quick survey of the archipelago, including a cursory inspection of two large islands some four miles north-west of the Graveyard. High Island (now East Wallabi) is the only one in the group that has a hillock – a bushy hump that rises some forty feet above sea level, presenting the only landmark visible from some distance at sea. From this too-hasty inspection, they concluded that the islands had no fresh water.

Pelsaert and Jacobsz knew that there was only one chance of rescue for the survivors: the VOC trading post in Java would have to be reached. The longboat was a mere open boat, some thirty feet long, sloop-rigged, with lee-boards in the Dutch fashion. Could such a frail sailing-boat manage a voyage of 1800 sea-miles (just over 3000 kilometres) across dangerous, uncharted waters? With experienced sailors, it might succeed. Only Jacobsz was sufficiently qualified to lead such a venture. Pelsaert, who could no longer trust his skipper, would need to come along to keep an eye on him, and they decided to take all the best sailors with them. To tell the others about this plan was out of the question: in their lawlessness and desperation they would all rush the longboat, which could carry only a very limited number of people. With its actual complement of forty-five, including two women (for Jacobsz had refused to abandon his Zwaantie) and one baby, it was already dangerously overloaded, and the carpenters had had to raise her freeboard in haste.

Therefore, four days after the shipwreck, the longboat hoisted sail at night and left silently, taking the yawl in tow. When, from their island, the castaways realised that their leaders had abandoned them, taking the only two boats, in their rage and despair they called the neighbouring islet, now deserted, Traitors' Island (*Verraderseiland*).

The Dutch shipbuilders were superb craftsmen. The wreck of the *Batavia* withstood the battering of the ocean for nine days. The agony of the ship had been long drawn-out, but her end came in a flash; she collapsed suddenly and her remains disappeared in a few moments. Of the seventy-odd men who had stayed on board, only twenty managed to reach land. For the last twenty-four hours, the former apothecary, Cornelisz, had taken refuge on the bowsprit where he clung, frozen in fear and drenched with spray. The bowsprit broke at the very end; Cornelisz could not swim but luckily fell into the sea amid a mass of planks and broken spars that the wind and the current brought to the shore of the Graveyard. He was the last of the *Batavia*'s survivors to reach land – he crawled ashore in a wretched state, terrified, exhausted, half-drowned.

The other castaways welcomed him warmly – all the more so because, in their depths of abandonment and despondency due to the desertion of their leaders, Cornelisz seemed to be the natural heir to lawful authority. Among the survivors he was the highest in the VOC hierarchy; he seemed the only one who could prevent them from sinking into lawlessness. These poor sheep thought that they had at last found a shepherd! Yet their tragic error is easy to understand. Cornelisz was a remarkable speaker; his eloquence exerted an almost irresistible power on those whom he wanted to seduce or direct, and in this case he was dealing with a crowd that was particularly vulnerable. Their latest ordeal had completely crushed their spirits. In their first days on the island, ten of them had already died. These deaths were apparently caused by thirst – an odd explanation since heavy showers had temporarily solved the water problem. It seems more likely that they died of sheer despair.

As soon as he had somewhat recovered, Cornelisz took up his new role with cool self-confidence. He allocated to himself the best tent and went about in Pelsaert's splendid finery. But at the same time, his first initiatives seemed to vindicate the trust his companions had placed in him: he succeeded in restoring some order, he harnessed all energies, he took stock of the available supplies and organised their distribution. Already the wretched mob around him began to experience new hope. They were only too happy to entrust their fate to a man who appeared so well-endowed with vision and authority. They had no misgivings when, a few weeks later, Cornelisz undertook a complete reorganisation of their small community. There was a fundamental rule in the VOC: all decisions had to be taken by a committee. Thus, very soon after the shipwreck, the survivors had chosen five people – the *predikant*, the surgeon and three others who enjoyed a certain prestige – to wield executive authority. Soon after reaching shore, Cornelisz was naturally invited to chair this committee. After a while, though, he suddenly decided to replace the five original members with individuals whose personal loyalty he had previously secured – plotters already recruited aboard the *Batavia* to carry out the mutiny he had planned with the skipper. The first decision of this new committee was to arrest and sentence to death a soldier charged with stealing wine from the stores. The sentence was carried out immediately. The harshness of this punishment may well have stunned the castaways, but they could still reason that extreme circumstances called for extreme measures – and besides, had not the judgment as well as the execution been carried out in accordance with the standing rules of the VOC?

Cornelisz's ultimate aim had not changed since plotting with the skipper to stage a mutiny on the *Batavia*. But after the shipwreck, his plan became far less realistic, for its success now hinged on new, highly problematic conditions. First, the *Commandeur* and the skipper had to reach Java with the longboat – a very hypothetical proposition. Then the VOC had to send a ship to rescue the castaways. And finally, the plotters had to gain mastery over that ship. This last point was crucial, but it was also fraught with the greatest risks. To carry it out, Cornelisz would have to get, if not the active support of all the survivors, at least their absolute obedience. When the rescue ship came, one single dissenter bent on disclosing the plot could ruin everything.

Cornelisz's first task was therefore to expand the network of the original plotters. After a while, he found himself at the head of two dozen mutineers and thugs, most of them very young men, quite a few of whom – cadets and mercenaries – could handle weapons. He had also recruited some sailors and even a VOC clerk, who became his deputy. He ordered all the weapons that had been salvaged from the ship – swords, axes, cutlasses and two muskets – to be gathered in one store to which he had sole access. Finally he reserved for himself exclusive use of the few makeshift boats and rafts that had been assembled with the timber recuperated from the wreck. To allow anyone free use of these crafts would have given the castaways too much autonomy. Carpenters from the ship had started to build a boat that would have been able to sail beyond the lagoon. Cornelisz ordered them to stop at once. Some time later, two of them were accused (rightly or wrongly) of having borrowed a small boat without authorisation. Cornelisz's new committee condemned them to death, and the sentence was carried out on the spot. These two new murders, public and legal, were committed without hesitation, despite the fact that the carpenters had skills that were crucial to the castaways in their present situation.

If, in the beginning, Cornelisz's initiatives answered some real needs of the shipwrecked community, his principal aim was nevertheless to strengthen his personal power. This particular objective soon became paramount. His actions became increasingly monstrous, but they were not irrational. In fact, they were dictated by an implacable logic: the need to retain and reinforce his absolute control over this little kingdom.

To start with, his main problem was that the mutineers were still a minority – about one-sixth of the total population of the island. To reverse this dangerous disproportion, he came up with a radical solution: to eliminate the surplus population. And from that point on, he applied all his cunning to achieve this objective.

Arguing that the Graveyard lacked space and resources, he organised a transfer of population to two other islets, promising the deported that they would enjoy better living conditions there. His real intention, in fact, was to abandon them where they would die of hunger and thirst. A small group was transported to Traitors' Island, the desolate rock near the place where the *Batavia* had sunk, and a second group, more numerous, to Seal Island, a long, sandy and narrow island facing the Graveyard on the other side of the deep water channel which crosses the archipelago.

And finally, on the pretext that it would be advantageous to explore the two large islands in the northwest, Cornelisz sent a party of some twenty men there. They were to investigate whether these islands might provide a more suitable environment for the eventual resettlement of the castaways (which would indeed have been a very wise decision, though it was not Cornelisz's true intention). He wanted particularly to get rid of this group; they were hardy and loyal soldiers who had spontaneously gathered round one of their own, a certain Wiebbe Hayes. Hayes was an ordinary soldier, but during the dramatic events and hardships they had just experienced he must have shown uncommon qualities of natural leadership, which had earned him the respect and trust of his comrades. Cornelisz had this small party dropped on the strand of High Island without food or weapons, promising that they would be brought back soon. In the meantime, they were to send out smoke signals if they found fresh water. But the former apothecary was convinced that the island was arid and without any resources; as before, his intention was simply to let them die of hunger and thirst, for he had rightly assessed that this group of men could eventually present the greatest impediment to his plans.

Shortly after the departure of Wiebbe Hayes and his team, Cornelisz managed to liquidate a few more people without awakening the suspicions of the others. Pretending that they had been sent to reinforce the explorers of the larger islands, he had them silently bludgeoned and drowned by his henchmen. But such piecemeal murders were not a satisfactory way of dealing with the problem; more drastic steps had to be taken.

It is at this point that something unforeseen occurred, which precipitated a dramatic development. Twenty days after Wiebbe Hayes and his companions had been left on High Island, smoke signals could be seen across the entire archipelago, indicating that they had found water. Cornelisz was appalled: not only were these potential trouble-makers still alive, but because they had water on their big island, they might even be prospering there, in impudent autonomy. For the other castaways, marooned on arid islets where their survival was at the mercy of irregular rainsqualls, these smoke signals brought sudden hope. This was especially true for the wretched people on Traitors' Island, whose situation had become desperate: they decided at once to go to this new Promised Land. With planks and spars retrieved from the wreck, they managed to assemble a few rafts that they immediately put to water.

Cornelisz saw this pitiful flotilla on its way towards the larger islands. Such spontaneous migration would not only strengthen Hayes' camp, it would also provide a dangerous example to the other survivors. This could not be tolerated; it had to be stopped at once otherwise his own authority might quickly unravel. He ordered his henchmen to intercept them with their larger and faster crafts.

Crowded on the shore, the population of the Graveyard watched the chase and witnessed its conclusion in horror. Cornelisz's thugs overtook the rafts easily and in cold blood slaughtered all those on board – men, women and children.

Cornelisz had finally shown his true colours – any ambiguity had vanished. He had power of life and death over the entire population of the islands, with the sole exception of Hayes and his team, who were now beyond his reach. On the Graveyard, a dozen castaways immediately drew their own conclusions and, on their own initiative, swore an oath of allegiance to the former apothecary. In the days that followed, Cornelisz ordered everyone to follow this example and swear the same oath. But this did not stop him from slaughtering his redundant subjects, beginning with the sick and the lame, who had been gathered in one tent. Then, from time to time, individual victims were selected at random, under various pretexts, or without any reason at all – for it is always its very arbitrariness that is the essence of an effective Terror. ('Here there is no *why*' was the answer given by the Auschwitz guards to the innocents they led to their deaths.) Only Cornelisz and his lieutenants decided who would live, who would die. Nobody was safe; it was imperative to show total obedience at all times – which did not guarantee what would happen the following day. Thus, for instance, the wretched *predikant*, who had seen his whole family butchered except for his eldest daughter (on whom Cornelisz's deputy had designs), fawned on his family's killers with a trembling submissiveness, swallowing his tears, living from day to day, striving for invisibility. Cornelisz had now styled himself 'Captain-General'. He and his crowd were a caste of lords: they had the best tents; they had at their disposal the women who had been spared because of their youth; they strutted about in fancy uniforms, bedecked with braids and ribbons; they drank the fine wines from the *Batavia*; they paraded about the island with swords, axes, cut-lasses and maces. Anyone who caught their attention had instantly to prove his submissiveness and swear fealty to the Captain-General. For instance, he might be shown a victim whom he was ordered to drown, brain, strangle or stab. If he wavered, the punishment was applied to him.

Thus all were eventually implicated in an endless cycle of killing. Ultimately, who was a murderer and who a victim? Cornelisz's aim was to erase the distinction between the two; his power was built on this very confusion. The oath of loyalty that everyone had sworn (and had to swear again several times) sanctioned their participation in the slaughter. There were also those who agreed to play an active and personal part in the murders. Though most of them killed simply because they were afraid of being killed themselves, some ended up developing a taste for it. One in particular, a puny teenager, begged to be allowed to cut some throats, a task for which he, in his debility, was ill-suited. Even his masters were somewhat taken aback by such a lust for blood.

A civilised society is not one in which the percentage of criminals and perverts is lower (the proportion must be about the same in all human communities); it is simply one that gives them less opportunity to indulge their inclinations. Without Cornelisz, his two dozen henchmen would probably never have shown – or even discovered – their true natures. There is no doubt that it was the personality of the former apothecary and the inspiration he imparted to his followers that made it possible to set up and sustain over a period of three months a weird and gruesome kingdom of murder amongst a population of two hundred and fifty decent individuals.

When all is said and done, Cornelisz himself remains an enigma. The diagnosis of modern psychology – which considers him a psychopath – is probably correct, but it does not explain him any better than the charge of heresy brought by his judges. They had in fact detected the mainspring of what must be called his genius. The strength, the steadfastness that sustained and motivated him – and enabled him to convince and lead a motley team of devoted disciples – sprang from his beliefs: his authority had an ideological basis. For the former apothecary did not otherwise cut a very impressive figure. He did not have the dash, the bold bearing with which great adventurers and conquerors win the blind allegiance of their partisans and subjugate simple and coarse people. On the contrary, on several occasions he showed himself to be surprisingly timorous. For example, he was so scared of water that he came close to drowning by hanging onto the wreck until the very last minute. He could order in cold blood the execution of countless atrocities but was squeamish when it came to performing the killings himself. Though personally responsible for more than a hundred and twenty savage and senseless murders, he attempted to kill only once, without success. Exasperated by the wails of an infant, he gave it poison but managed only to put it into a coma, and had to ask an underling to finish off the job he had botched.

On another occasion he organised the collective rape of the women whose lives had been spared (while two-thirds were liquidated, the rest were put at the disposal of the mutineers), but displayed an odd timidity when it came to gratifying his own yearnings. Two women had been kept from his henchmen: the *predikant*'s eldest daughter, whom Cornelisz's lieutenant had forced to become his 'fiancée', and the beautiful Lucretia, whom Cornelisz reserved for himself, settling her in his tent. Lucretia, however, resisted him for twelve days. Humiliated by her rebuffs, Cornelisz confessed his frustration to his deputy – the former VOC clerk, by now the most ferocious killer of the gang. The clerk wondered how such a simple matter could even be a problem. He immediately went to see Lucretia and reminded her of the only choice before her: either she would comply with the Captain-General's demands or she would share the fate of the other women and be strangled or prostituted to a pack of murderers. On the same day, Lucretia became Cornelisz's 'concubine'.

Cornelisz's character is puzzling: his personality is difficult to define, his features remain hazy. At times he was unable to face events, or to take action in the face of pressing dangers. And yet, as we've seen (and we shall return to this), his powers of persuasion were so extraordinary that he trusted in them blindly. His eloquence did not work in a void; it was not the mere agility of a sophist, but rather drew on the inner resources of an ideology. His judges were struck by the fact that at the core of his stubborn resilience was a staunch belief in a doctrine which they simply deemed to be heretical but never attempted to clearly describe. For us today, this doctrine is even more difficult to grasp. Only two clues, equally vague and ambiguous, remain to guide our conjectures.

First, there is the Torrentius connection. Cornelisz claimed to be his disciple; he had been close to the painter, and it is this fact that attracted the attention of the investigating authorities, forcing him to change his career suddenly and escape overseas.

But who was Torrentius, and what were his ideas? His contemporaries portray him as an utterly loathsome and immoral character. He revelled in deliberately offending the values and beliefs of decent and respectable people; sacrilege, lechery, drunkenness and blasphemy were his favourite pastimes. Did his scandalous public statements reflect his actual philosophy, or did he take pleasure in shocking the narrow conventions of a bourgeois society? Did he believe what he proclaimed, or were his outrageous paradoxes merely for goading the fools? In his time, art-lovers and critics thought him an artist of genius – and in the golden age of Dutch painting, local connoisseurs knew what they were talking about. Torrentius boasted that he painted with the personal help of the Devil, and the super-human beauty of his art lends some credit to this claim. An atheist is the exact opposite of a follower of Satan, but in what camp did Torrentius place himself? For he also alleged that Hell was but a silly superstition …

He was ultimately arrested in 1627 (some ten months before the *Batavia* set sail) and charged with the crimes of heresy and immorality. He was also suspected of belonging to the secret society of Rosicrucians. The prosecutor asked for the death penalty, but despite having undergone torture, Torrentius remained steadfast and refused to confess his guilt. To this he owed his life, but he was condemned to twenty years' imprisonment. King Charles I of England, who was a Maecenas and knowledgeable art-collector (perhaps the only English monarch ever to show a true appreciation of art!), interceded personally on his behalf to the Prince of Orange and obtained his early release two years later. Torrentius was granted his freedom only under the strict condition that he leave for England immediately, never to return to the Netherlands. He spent about a dozen years at the English court where he caused 'more scandal than satisfaction' and 'painted very little'. (Just like the luminous Vermeer, of whom he was a kind of obverse, dark figure, the perfectionism of his pictorial manner precluded the possibility of abundant production.) During the troubles that marked the end of Charles I's reign (before the King was brought to the scaffold), Torrentius lost his royal pension. Without employment, he returned in secret to Holland where he was once again arrested and tortured. He died in 1644, free – it seems – but destitute.

It would be futile to speak of a great painter without being able to refer to his works. In the case of Torrentius, one of his paintings miraculously survived, and it is truly a masterpiece. Everything he had painted in the Netherlands was confiscated and burnt by judicial order when he was condemned. As for the few works he completed in England, it was long thought that they had disappeared after the sale and dispersal of the royal collection that followed the fall of Charles I. But in fact one of them, which was probably brought to Holland in the nineteenth century, became the property of a wholesale grocer in a provincial town. An art historian discovered it by chance in 1913 and identified it – the reverse side of the panel still bears the seal of Charles I. At the time, the grocer's heirs used it in their shop as a lid to cover a barrel of sultanas.

This painting (beautifully restored), *Still Life with a Bridle,* now hangs in the Rijksmuseum in Amsterdam. To what extent can we rely on it to trace the painter's ideas? We may as well try to solve an enigma by means of a riddle. The painting occupies a circular space within an octagonal frame. Its composition – complex though harmonious and serene – presents a juxtaposition of symbolic objects: a water jug, a wine pitcher, a glass, two pipes, a sheet of music with notes and words, and a bridle. Each element is depicted with eerie accuracy which suggests the grain and texture of the different materials – glass, tin, clay, paper, ceramic, metal. This arrangement of disparate utensils and props forms one visual metaphor, whose key eludes us. The bridle, hanging in the background shadows where only the iron bits gleam faintly, dominates the entire composition. Though it can barely be seen, it sums up the allegorical subject of the painting: Temperance (a

theme not lacking in irony considering the artist's noto-
riously flamboyant debauchery). The smooth painted
surface bears no trace of brushstrokes: forms, volumes
and light are made visible through the invisible magic
of a virtuoso execution. The perfection of the whole is
unsettling. The background is black, but not opaque; it
is rather like a dark mirror of still water at the bottom
of a well over which the onlooker leans in vain. The
painting communicates a sense of plenitude but keeps
its secret sealed.

The other mainspring of Cornelisz's mind is – without doubt – anabaptism. Anabaptism is a heresy with a
long history. It took diverse forms, some of which were
violent, in Germany and the Netherlands. Cornelisz
was born into a family that belonged to one of these
sects, and had therefore never been baptised. After
being sentenced to death, he pretended that he wanted
baptism, thus hoping to delay the execution indefi-
nitely. But when he saw that it would bring him only a
few hours' respite, he reverted to his heresy.

The exact nature of his anabaptism is difficult to
define. In some of its branches the doctrine followed
an austere and mystic path, yet it also spawned various sects that cultivated esoteric, violent or orgiastic
practices. One thinks of the Adamites, for instance:

nearly a century before the wreck of the *Batavia*, Hieronymus Bosch depicted their suave and poisonous mysteries in his *Garden of Delights*, a disquieting nudist revelry hovering between Heaven and Hell, in a limbo of improbable innocence[†]. The common feature of all these sects was their denial of the doctrine of the Fall and the knowledge of good and evil. We may note in passing that, oddly enough, it is people who do not believe in Hell who often create good imitations of it here on earth.

In about mid-July, Cornelisz sent his executioners to kill off the population of Seal Island – some forty people, mostly women and children (ships' boys and other young servants) but also a dozen adult men. Believing that this wretched crowd had been suitably weakened by their long exile on an arid and sandy bank, Cornelisz thought that half a dozen men would be enough for the

---

[†]   In the famous and enigmatic triptych which hangs in the Prado, the central panel describes these gloomy "delights" (one could easily believe that the sixteenth century already knew of the resorts for erotomaniacs which Michel Houellebecq describes so well), while the left panel shows the Earthly Paradise, and the right panel shows Hell. The ambiguities of this cryptic painting have given rise to countless attempts at exegesis; the most convincing interpretation seems to be that the central panel refers to the ritual orgies of an Adamite sect of 's Hertogenbosch.

job. However, in the confusion of the attack, seven castaways managed to escape, and reached Hayes' island on makeshift rafts. In the following weeks, in groups of twos and threes, several more inhabitants of the Graveyard deserted Cornelisz's camp and followed the same escape route, swimming or drifting across the lagoon, hanging on to planks or broken spars.

Thus Hayes ended up with about fifty men in his camp. The new arrivals told him all about the atrocities organised by Cornelisz and his gang, and he realised that any agreement with such an enemy was unthinkable. Cornelisz had sent a messenger in a sham diplomatic approach, but clearly he was going to attack sooner or later. This invasion appeared all the more certain since the balance of power was turning more and more to Hayes' advantage. Though Cornelisz had all the supplies, weapons and equipment salvaged from the wreck, Hayes and his men enjoyed a much more favourable natural environment. Their two islands, where the *Commandeur* and the skipper should have settled the survivors from the very beginning, were not only much larger, but also had unlimited resources: fresh water wells created by the seepage of rainwater over hundreds of years; an abundant fauna; small scrub wallabies, *tammars*, easy to catch, and whose meat is delicious; thousands of sea-birds nesting on the ground, which can be caught by hand while they are sitting on their nests full of eggs. Better still, the waters around the islands were teeming with sea life, more than anywhere else on the archipelago. (Today, for four months every year, they are fished for crayfish. While I was there, I ate the same meals as the fishermen, and I can assure you that crayfish for breakfast is hardly a pauper's fare).

We have no information about Hayes, except that he was a soldier – a private – from a small town in Groningen. We know him only through what he did, and what he did bears witness to his strength of character and his military ability: he had natural authority, good judgment and courage. Is such a cluster of qualities so rare? Yes, if we consider that out of three hundred survivors of the *Batavia*, there was only one Hayes. But once he had stepped out of obscurity, he became a rallying point, and a growing number of volunteers joined him. The will, the discipline and the resourcefulness of that group presented a decisive obstacle to Cornelisz's ambition and were eventually to cause his downfall.

Cornelisz had understood straightaway that the very existence of Hayes and his troop was a challenge to his rule, and could not be allowed to continue. He should therefore have acted quickly to eliminate this menace. Yet, following the successful escape of the group of castaways from Seal Island, he wasted two weeks dithering. He may well have been held back by fear.

Hayes, meanwhile, used the time to organise the defence of his island. He improvised weapons: cudgels, pikes, planks with long carpenter's nails driven through them. On top of a slope, which the attackers had to climb after landing and crossing the coral shallows, he used dry stones to build a small fort – four low walls forming a square, judiciously erected near a fresh water well.[†] Within this enclosure, his men piled up a large heap of heavy and sharp pieces of rock to hurl at the attackers should they attempt to storm the fort.

At the beginning of August, Cornelisz's troop made two attempts to land. Both times, they were repelled. They had better weapons, but there were fewer of them; by now the Captain-General had only some twenty seasoned killers at his disposal against Hayes' fifty men. The latter group had only makeshift weapons, but they were better fed and, more importantly, they had the moral advantage – the desperate determi-

---

[†]   This fort and the well can still be seen today.

nation that can inspire decent men when they find themselves cornered by an unjust aggressor and have to fight for their lives.

Cornelisz decided to lead a third attempt himself. Blinded by a mad belief in the powers of his eloquence, he thought that by directly addressing Hayes' partisans, he would be able to sow dissent among them. This plan collapsed in a rout: Cornelisz was taken alive and his three best lieutenants had their heads smashed. As a result of this unexpected disaster, the rest of the mutineers fled in panic and returned to the Graveyard.

Without their leader, Cornelisz's gang was, literally, headless. Certainly, there were still a few crazed killers among them but, strangely enough, these were spurned as candidates for the leadership by most of the mutineers, who instead replaced Cornelisz with a young soldier who had professional competence but was not a confirmed criminal. (Once, in an unprecedented move, he had even quietly refused to perform an execution ordered by Cornelisz.) And indeed, under his leadership, blood ceased to flow on the Graveyard.

But on 17 September– a crucial date in the story of *Batavia*'s survivors – he launched a new attack on Hayes' island. This time the campaign took a dangerous turn. From the start, the assailants made devastating use of the two muskets that had been salvaged from the ship. The efficiency of these weapons was limited only by their slow rate of fire, but by taking time one could use them to kill from a distance an enemy who had absolutely no means of retaliation. Three defenders had already fallen without being able to counterattack when suddenly – and here the story's ending seems to come from a Hollywood screenwriter – a sail appeared on the horizon: Pelsaert was back, coming to the rescue with a small, fast VOC ship!

The longboat had taken a month to reach Java; the journey had been dangerous and full of hardships. The people on board had endured hunger and thirst but everyone survived, including the baby. To justify his desertion, Pelsaert had to give some rather delicate explanations to the authorities. Not unreasonably, he managed to deflect the ire of his superiors onto the skipper, who was swiftly flung into a cell from which he would never come out alive. The authorities then ordered Pelsaert to return to the Abrolhos to bring back the survivors, as well as all that could be retrieved from the *Batavia's* precious cargo. For this he was given the light 'jacht' *Sardam*, with her skipper, a crew of twenty-five and a team of divers.

Despite contrary winds, the *Sardam* took only three weeks to retrace the longboat's route. Once in the vicinity of the Abrolhos, however, the rescue party lost an entire month trying to locate the exact position of the archipelago. Not only did they ignore its longitude, but the skipper, after the shipwreck, had miscalculated its latitude! The islands are so low on the water that they are only visible at close range, and thus the *Sardam* had to execute endless zigzags before eventually finding them.

Among the mutineers, only a handful of fanatics tried to carry out Cornelisz's original plan of taking over the *Sardam*. This attempt, hastily improvised in a moment of panic, was so harebrained – even Cornelisz's successor refused to take part in it – that it petered out immediately. Pelsaert, who had not only the crew of *Sardam* on his side but also Hayes' men, managed to capture the whole gang without a fight.

Without wasting any time, Pelsaert put Cornelisz and his main accomplices on trial on the spot. To get their full confessions, as required by Dutch law, he had to subject the accused to torture. The criminal atrocities of the last three months were thus followed by legal atrocities. Cornelisz, torn between his fear of torture and an impudent determination to maintain his absolute innocence, caused his judges (Pelsaert and the senior staff of the *Sardam*) much trouble. He confessed and then recanted, by turn.

In the end he was condemned to hang with six of his accomplices. The court also decided that his two hands would be amputated before he was hanged. The executions took place on 2 October, on Seal Island, where erecting a scaffold was easier because the sandy ground was soft. The day before the hanging, Cornelisz, who had managed to get hold of poison – it was never found out how – tried to kill himself. Either because the dose was too small or because the poison had lost its power, it merely induced a dreadful colic, and he spent his last night vomiting, and with continuous diarrhoea.

The accomplices had requested that Cornelisz be the first to die. They knew their former chief and feared that, at the last moment, he might pull off some new trick and evade their common fate. With his two hands cut off, Cornelisz's death must have been swift: loss of blood would have killed him before asphyxiation. The others endured their final agony in its terrible slowness. In a modern hanging, as the condemned falls through a trap, his neck vertebrae are dislocated and death is instantaneous. But in earlier times death was caused by progressive strangulation; the instinctive and grotesque movements of the hanged, which slowed or hastened the tightening of the hanging knot, turned this type of execution into a show that was much appreciated by the mob as well as by polite society.[†]

If one is to believe the testimony of the *predikant* – whose assistance Cornelisz refused – the former apothecary's last words were 'Revenge! Revenge!' One may well appreciate Pelsaert's relief after the execution; a heavy burden had been taken off his shoulders. He would have dreaded being at sea for another month with this diabolical apothecary on board. Even in chains, what new mischief could he not have caused?

This matter now settled, Pelsaert spent the next six weeks attending to his superiors' principal concern: salvaging the *Batavia*'s treasure. Not only did he manage to retrieve nine chests filled with silver, but in his scrupulous zeal he went even further: in an attempt to recover a small barrel of vinegar, of little value, a boat with five men on board was carried away by a sudden squall, and lost forever.

[†] A century later, for instance, in a letter written to his sister from Milan, the young Mozart – he was fifteen at the time – tells how he had enjoyed watching 'four rascals being hanged in the Duomo Square' and recalls that, four years before, he had found the same entertainment in Lyons.

On 15 November 1629, the *Sardam* left the Abrolhos Islands for good. Pelsaert was bringing back to Batavia seventy survivors, sixteen of whom were criminals in irons. On the way, he dropped two of them on the coast of the Australian mainland. He had commuted their death sentences, but could well have suspected that the VOC worthies would not approve of such clemency. One of the two was Cornelisz's successor who, once in power, had stopped the killings. The other was the teenager who had begged to be allowed to kill – his tender age seemed to mitigate his guilt. They were both left on an empty beach. Though they did not land there of their own free will, these two murderers can well be considered the very first European settlers in Australia. They received a bag full of baubles, trinkets and little wooden toys called *Nurenbergen* (from the town where they were made), to help them establish friendly relations with the natives, should they encounter any. Nobody knows what happened to them: they were swallowed by the bush and never seen again.

Once in Batavia, Pelsaert handed the remaining fourteen convicts to the authorities, who lost no time in hanging five of them and submitting the others to torture.

The only hero of this entire story, Wiebbe Hayes,

was promoted to the rank of standard-bearer, with a significant increase in pay. The news of this promotion is also the last time he is mentioned in the archives; nothing is known of his subsequent fate.

As for Lucretia, she had been the victim of obscene aggression, then shipwrecked, and then raped and forced to become the concubine of a murderous maniac. When she finally landed in Batavia, it was only to learn that she had become a widow: her husband had died just two months before from a tropical fever in Burma. Still beautiful, it seems, she married a military man the following year. Five years later, the couple went back to the Netherlands and we lose track of her. It could well be that she died in Amsterdam in 1681, at nearly eighty years of age; the identification is not certain, but plausible. This woman obviously had a gift for survival – which, after all, is another form of heroism.

*

In spite of the hardships and the deprivation he had suffered, Robinson Crusoe shed tears on leaving his island. One can understand how he felt. I spent only a fortnight on the Abrolhos, but I would gladly have stayed six months. I had not been shipwrecked, of course. Nevertheless, if the *Batavia*'s survivors had organised themselves without Cornelisz and exploited the resources of the two large islands and of the lagoon, they might have enjoyed not only a peaceful life, but even something akin to happiness. Though the islands are quite arid and windswept, the climate is mild. Rain-squalls often occur in winter, but the breeze is never cold and the sun is quick to return. Then, when the blues of sky and sea meet, the whole archipelago is transformed: swallowed by light, it seems to dissolve in infinity.

Today the archipelago is still uninhabited, except during the crayfish season. Around the end of March, fishing boats from the continent come to the islands. The fishermen have established ashore what they call their 'camps', where they stay each year for three or four months; these are makeshift huts, semi-permanent constructions built mainly of corrugated iron sheets and fibro-concrete boards. They have set moorings for their boats in the rare spots where the water is both deep and sheltered, and to stay as near to these boats as possible most of their shacks are crowded on two islets so tiny that the *Batavia*'s survivors had completely neglected them. Some fifty years ago, a commercial company extracting guano scraped the rocks to the bone and now every square foot of this lunar surface is covered by the flimsy and haphazard structures of the fishermen's slum. Half a dozen of them, however, have chosen to live away from the crowd and set their camps on Beacon Island – the notorious 'Batavia's Graveyard'. This is where I stayed.

The whole archipelago is a nature reserve, strictly protected. As a rule, tourists and visitors are not admitted unless as a fisherman's guests. My host, Bruce D., was a sixty-year-old veteran. Crippled by arthritis, and with failing eyesight (he would not appreciate my description because when he came to visit in Sydney the following year, he was proud to show us his latest girlfriend, a young and charming hairdressing salon manager), he was past retirement age, but as he owned his boat, every year he followed the irresistible call of the new season. I don't think he had to do this for financial reasons. This sort of fishing is hard work, but the men remain free nine months of the year, and each season brings them a small fortune. Bruce could easily have decided to take a rest. Was it the comradeship of work that brought him back to the islands – or the islands themselves?

It was the full southern winter, near the end of June, and the fishing season was coming to a close. Almost all of the other fishermen had gone back to the

mainland. A few remained on Beacon Island: Bruce –
who said he was there for a few more days to make
some repairs to his hut – and a young couple, Rod and
Barbara, whose camp was at the other end of the island.
Rod and Barbara had been married for a year, but they
still behaved like newlyweds. In a society ruled by harsh
conventions compelling men to be laconic and tough,
where all displays of emotions are considered a shame-
ful sign of weakness, it was remarkable that Rod was
not afraid to demonstrate his affection for his young
wife. A good sailor, he had a large boat with superb
electronic navigation equipment; at the very end of the
season, he seemed to fish for pleasure, mostly enjoying
these last days of being alone with Barbara.

Using either Bruce's or Rod's boat, the four of us
often went out to set and raise the lobster-pots, or we
sailed outside the lagoon, dragging lines with big hooks
in the hope of catching a shark or a marlin; or we
explored the larger islands of the archipelago, taking a
dinghy in tow to land on the strands. In the evenings,
after dinner, using electricity from a noisy diesel engine,
we watched pleasantly silly movies, can of beer in hand,
till we fell asleep, suddenly exhausted by a day of sun,
wind and sea.

So time went by; there seemed to be only one long

day, white, then blue, as when one crosses an ocean on a ship … And then came the day when it was time for me to go back to the mainland. As I was packing my bag, Bruce said: 'Well, before you leave …' He hesitated briefly, then continued: 'Never mind, I'll show it to you, but you must promise me you won't tell anyone, or I'll be in trouble.' From the shelf above the larder he took down a purple plastic ice-cream container, one of the three-litre kind sold in supermarkets. He put it on the table and removed the lid. Inside was a human skull, yellowed by age. 'Last month, to enlarge the kitchen, I started to dig the ground before casting the cement, when I discovered two skeletons. I only kept this thing and poured the concrete over the rest. They're under our feet now,' he said, and pointed at the kitchen's new cement floor. 'But, please! Not a word about this – otherwise, I'll have the police coming here from the mainland, and the archaeologists and all the rest, and they'll mess up my entire kitchen!' Then with a grin he shut the purple container and put it back on the shelf, between the vinegar and the tomato sauce.[†]

[†] I don't think I am betraying the trust of my host. My visit took place sixteen years ago; I hope 'Bruce D.' (not his real name) is still alive, but I doubt very much if he still has a 'camp' on Beacon Island.

It was time to leave. Outside, the weather was glorious. Here the beautiful winter days have a mildness that European summers seldom do. Muffled by distance, the monotonous thunder of the breakers exploding on the reef set off the silence. Right then it was suddenly obvious to me: this story of the *Batavia*'s survivors must be told. But how? I only knew that it should start with a verse from *Iphigenia in Tauris* that had stuck in my mind since I came to the islands:

The sea washes away the evils of men.

PROSPER

By all that's wonderful, it is the sea, I believe, the sea itself –
or is it youth alone? Who can tell? But you here – you all had
something out of life: money, love – whatever one gets on shore
– and, tell me, wasn't that the best time, that time when we
were young at sea; young and had nothing, on the sea that
gives nothing, except hard knocks – and sometimes a chance
to feel your strength – that only – what you all regret?
—JOSEPH CONRAD, *Youth*

When I was a student, during my last summer in Europe before I left for the Far East, I had an opportunity to join the crew of a tuna-fishing boat from Brittany – one of the last boats working under sail.

Sorting out some papers recently, I came across the notes I had taken then – some forty-five years ago – about this experience of my youth.

The following narrative is based on these notes, but I have not modified their contents, for these memories are dear to me and they evoke a world that no longer exists.

Prosper and *Étoile de France* leaving Etel on a fishing trip (1958).

By train to Auray. It seems that true Brittany starts only now, as I leave the railway station and take the bus to Etel.

It is Assumption Day. The Breton women went to Mass this morning and will go back to church for Vespers in the afternoon, while their men spend the day in the cafés. The bus is full of women in long black skirts and white lace head-dresses. There are a few sailors wearing their Sunday best; a priest, built like a woodcutter, is reading his breviary. The bus has to stop on the way to allow a drunken sailor to piss on the side of the road. The women crack a few jokes – spiced with rough peasant wit – at his expense. First contact with the Breton drunks: I shall get to know them better later on. But why do the French say 'drunk as all Poland' when they have Brittany so much closer to hand?

The road winds through verdant countryside, offering brief views whenever it reaches the top of a short, steep rise; but most of the time, green hedges and grey walls screen off the landscape and turn it into a maze of secret corners. Now and then I see stone villages with their slate roofs sitting tight under stunted trees. I have not been here before, but I feel almost at home.

*

In its heyday, Etel had a tuna-fishing fleet of nearly two hundred sailing boats – yawls, ketches and cutters – but these were progressively replaced by motor vessels, and now only two yawls remain: *Prosper* and *Étoile de France*.

I had been told that the owner-skipper of *Prosper*, Monsieur Pessel, sometimes agreed to take a passenger on board. He confirmed this to me by letter in the spring. His letter was short and rather non-committal. He simply suggested that I come and see him in the summer, between two *marées*.[†]

[†]   Each fishing trip is called a 'marée'.

When I arrive in Etel, the skipper, who has returned only a few days earlier, is playing *boules* with some friends. Seeing me, he seems annoyed and somewhat nonplussed. It is obvious that he has forgotten his vague promise (and, as I am to discover later on, he has already granted the same favour to another candidate). Most of all, he is keen to resume his game of *boules*. After hesitating briefly, he shrugs: 'All right, drop your bag on board. We leave the day after tomorrow. This *marée* will be long, probably a month.' And with that, he turns back to his game.

*

Louis, a crewman from *Prosper* whom I'd met earlier in the harbour, introduced me to the skipper. Now that I have been accepted, he offers to show me the boat. This takes time: our course is cunningly plotted to allow us to call in at all the cafés in town. There, with the compulsory glasses of rough red wine, are laid the foundations of a staunch friendship.

Louis has no family. Staying ashore is fatal for him; in port, he stops drinking only when he sinks into sleep. Since he has been doing this for years, he is never truly drunk – just permanently soaked in drink. He is always blinking as if the light hurts his eyes. His head shakes.

One expects him to fall asleep at any moment. He hardly eats: red wine for him is as milk to the babe. He floats in a state of universal benevolence, but in fact he is not fully present. His amiable semi-absence is in marked contrast to the rowdy boisterousness of his fellow crewmen. For instance, when one jokingly refers to the wife who left him, Louis responds with a tolerant half-smile – but one feels that he detached himself from this business long ago.

However, he is a fine sailor, and in this he sums up the contradictions of the crew of *Prosper*. Very few fishermen are still willing to work under sail. This type of fishing is difficult, hazardous and less efficient. The skipper, therefore, can only recruit wrecks like Louis, or other men who can no longer sustain the relentless rhythm of work on the motor boats. Yet men who can handle sail are becoming rare, and in this respect *Prosper*'s crew belongs to a true elite – the last group to maintain the traditions of what is a supreme form of seamanship.

This year, at the end of spring, when boats are prepared for the tuna season, Louis was almost prevented from embarking. At the *Inscription maritime*'s compulsory medical inspection he was found physically unfit and duly rejected. This might have forced him into a vicious cycle: he can escape alcoholism only if he sails, but because of his alcoholism he is forbidden to go to sea. The skipper was in a quandary: first, because finding a replacement would not be easy; and second, because he was afraid of the consequences for Louis. The solution he finally found was to put Louis down on the crew's list as 'passenger'.

*

Right now, since *Étoile de France* is still at sea, *Prosper* is the only sailing boat in the harbour. At the quay, among the massive, ungainly *pinasses*, she alone belongs to another breed, like a stag among cattle. Low on the water, with her long, slender hull, her tall main-mast surging out of an ordered mess of stays, shrouds and halyards, she cuts an impressive figure. An expert's eye would trace her to the Camaret boatyard, where she was born twenty years ago. The line and slimness of her stern-post clearly signal her origins and make her, despite her size and weight, a boat as fast and as responsive to the helm as a yacht. The deck is completely clear to allow room for manoeuvring, and there are only two hatchways: one before the mast, providing access to the fish and sail holds, and one just for'ard of the helm, leading to the quarters.

Once on board, we hear a great deal of noise interspersed with sonorous swearing from the quarters. I go down to meet Robert – but the acquaintanceship is not mutual: right now he seems incapable of knowing anything, even how to put on a pair of trousers. This jolly, dishevelled giant is celebrating his thirty-second birthday, but in his drunken euphoria he absent-mindedly pissed in his pants and has had to come back on board to change clothes. This is made all the more difficult because he tries to get into his clean trousers by putting both legs in one trouser-leg. In his underpants, he hops on one foot, bumps his head against the low ceiling, falls on his backside, all the while furiously trying to swear, for, even when sober, he stutters.

While Louis goes for'ard to get a litre of red wine to clear his head, I look around the quarters. It is a low and dark room. One descends using a steep ladder, the only light provided by the opening of the hatchway. A table is fixed to the bulkhead and a bench runs around the three other sides, which gape with four dark openings. These are the 'hutches' or 'cribs', where the men sleep. In each of these hutches, which allow one to only sit or lie down, there is room for a large straw mattress. Only the skipper and old Félix have a crib to themselves; the others sleep two by two, and even manage to squeeze their baskets between the bulkhead and the mattress – in these baskets are individual food stores that contain each man's provision of butter, dry sausage and cheese.

The quarters are the heart of the boat. This is where we sleep, eat, spin yarns and live together. Even in port, when the boat is deserted, there are reminders everywhere of the crew's living presence: the heavy sea clothes, woollens, oilskins, sou'westers thrown on the benches; sea boots and wooden clogs piled up in a corner; each man's enamel coffee-mug hanging on a hook. On the table lies *L'Almanach du marin breton*, an empty bottle, some tobacco and a knife. The whole place smells of stale wine, fish, rubber clothes and damp straw.

Having managed to put on his trousers, Robert wants us to go out with him for a drink. But Louis has decided to be good; this evening he will stay with me on board, he will not go round the cafés again. Robert climbs on deck. The tread of his footsteps grows faint. Miraculously, he finds the quay ladder.

Louis opens a tin of bully-beef and fetches another litre of wine from the barrel. Under the light of a kerosene lamp, with a piece of bread in one hand and a knife in the other, we dig in.

After the meal, Louis finishes the wine, and launches into a long monologue which I will hear often. He is rather taciturn by nature, but after the last litre of the day he oozes a sort of diffuse bliss and relates to me the marvels of life on board. For him, the boat is everything: his home, his family, his refuge. 'You see, Pierre, we are not savages. On board, it is a sort of family life. You call me Louis, I call you Pierre. Of course, we tell each other off sometimes. Robert says to me, "you give me the shits," and I tell him to "bugger off," but that is because of the job: we have to. Because here we are not savages. We have the good life, the family life ...' On this theme, he can talk forever; even if he repeats the same things over and over again, the topic is inexhaustible, he will always think about it with wonder. He is right.

Imagine six men living together in a cramped space, never alone, each knowing everything about his companions, down to those humbling truths which, ashore, even one's closest friends might never become aware of: who is lazy, who is a coward, who is greedy, who snores, who is boastful, who is clumsy, whose wife is unfaithful. They exchange the same jokes, the same tales ... The fact is, they share the same experiences, they've had the same life: the sea since the age of thirteen, the

74

mean sea that begrudges them its fish, the weather so seldom kind, and chance always so stingy with its smiles – hasn't this been their common lot?

Most have had a brother, an uncle, a cousin or another relative 'lost at sea'. And every time a boat is lost, someone will remember having sailed on her; most will have had old friends among the crew. Nevertheless, they are fatalistic, they sail again. Their lot has been cast once and for all. They cannot escape it, this sea community, even ashore. Their little town with its heavy stone houses, just dumped in a bay on the Breton coast, faces the sea, lives with it, lives for it. High up on the hill, the rumble of the fish factory seems to echo the sounds of the harbour down below. And when the factory spews its boiling water along the gutters, the whole town reeks of fish.

In the main street, those who return from the sea pass those who prepare to go out. The former steer a zigzag course from café to café, recounting at every stop the story of their trip. The latter carry their baskets loaded with jars of butter and dry cakes, or stagger under a mattress of fresh straw.

The women, without ever having gone to sea, know its language. They know about the boats, and about winds and tides, they can read the signs of the weather;

their thoughts closely follow those who are out. On the church porch after mass, in the shops, on street corners, there is less talk about what happens 'in France' than about news from the sea, the sea that is more present in this town than the hard rock upon which it is built. 'Have you heard? *Belle-Monique* has collided with a cargo-boat in St George Channel. They say that the skipper is missing … *Étoile de France* is not back yet; they have now been out for thirty-five days. They have probably gone too far south and can't catch a return wind. Do you remember? *L'Espoir des Familles* had the same mishap some years ago; when they finally got home, they said they hadn't had bread for ten days and were forced to open their biscuit supplies … *Douce-Amélie* came back this morning with thirteen hundred tuna! Nearly all of them were caught in the last five days: they are always lucky. Ah well, this boat is *pêchant*, we all know that …'

Some elders – the skipper of the tug, the master of the ferry – are the custodians of a still higher tradition, and can talk about their youthful adventures sailing on the big square-riggers, three-masted barques and ships from Nantes that went round the Horn to fetch Chilean nitrates …

*

On board *Prosper*, the last preparations for departure are made. Ice is taken aboard as well as fresh food supplies, bread and wine. We leave tomorrow with the dawn tide. To leave later is unthinkable: the crew must not have time to get drunk before embarking. (It was exactly the same in Ostend, when I sailed on the Iceland trawlers.)

That night, around one o'clock, half-asleep, I vaguely hear footsteps on deck and some voices. But what wakes me up for good is a powerful shout from Robert: 'Don't make such a bloody noise! Pierre is sleeping down there!' And then, missing the first step, he falls off the ladder and rolls down to my crib with the clattering tumult of a mountain avalanche. Louis, more somnolent than ever, follows, stumbling at every rung, but he doesn't fall. (Drink may have ruined his health, but it has not impaired his sailor's balance. I have seen him climbing the mast or manoeuvring on the jib-boom in heavy weather with a kind of haggard precision, while on land he would not have been able to walk straight.) With them are two mates from another boat, here to drink to the impending departure. Louis goes for'ard to fetch some litres of wine. This is his official job – every day he must fill the crew's individual bottles by siphoning wine from the barrel in the hold with a long rubber tube, which he sucks on with more energy than is strictly required by the laws of physics.

They extract me from my hutch with the peculiar obstinacy of drunks who must eliminate all traces of sobriety in their vicinity. Robert wants to start a speech. His efforts to overcome his stuttering make his eyes roll and his veins bulge: one doesn't know whether he is going to tell a joke or start a row. Louis is silent; his dim eyes stare into emptiness. One of the visitors tells an endless tale of smuggling and shipwreck, to which nobody – not even he himself – pays any attention. In the end, the visitors leave. Only Louis remains. He takes the last bottle by the neck, empties it in one long gulp, collapses on the nearest mattress – the skipper's – like a stricken ox in a slaughterhouse, and begins to snore.

When I open my eyes, a square of grey day is visible through the hatch. The quarters are empty, and I hear footsteps above my head. Oh, the sounds of a good wooden boat getting ready to sail! Clogs and sea-boots hurrying on deck revive forgotten echoes in a hull that has been silent for days, motionless in port.

The whole crew is there, fresh and fit, including Robert and Louis: the sea awaits them, they are new

SIMON LEYS

men. Seven pairs of hands – from the skipper's to the boy's – haul out the boat still on her mooring lines, to bring her head into the wind in order to hoist the mainsail. The mainsail is huge and heavy – its gaff alone weighs as much as a young tree; hence, the only concession to mechanisation on these sail-fishing crafts is a motor windlass. But, because none among the crew is able to look after these motors, mishaps are frequent, and the story even goes that on one of the first boats equipped with such a windlass, the engine that had been started in port to hoist the mainsail ran continuously for a whole day till it eventually died from lack of fuel, because nobody on board knew how to turn it off.

For the moment, though, on *Prosper*, the question is not how to stop it, but how to start it. Louis is entrusted with all matters pertaining to the engine. Why Louis? Perhaps because he is in charge of getting the wine, and the barrel and the engine are in the same hold?

Louis disappears into the darkness of the for'ard hold, and a few moments later the engine starts with vigorous bangs, but also disheartening hiccups. Each time the mainsail halyard is engaged on the windlass, the engine stalls, like a shirking mule. Swearing follows, and everyone volunteers his opinion. The spark-

79

plug? The fuel intake? From time to time, Louis' head appears at the hatch, just to give a soothing forecast and announce another try. Of course, it would have been sensible to test the engine once or twice in advance, or to ask a competent technician to check it. But we are on a sailing boat; it was already a lot to ask to install such a contraption in the first place. To have to take care of it now (and to have to pay for such maintenance, for the skipper is stingy!) is really beyond the limit. In any case, the skipper, who is a superb seaman under sail, knows nothing about engines, and he resents having to hear Robert or Louis showing off their phoney mechanical expertise. Deep down, I suspect he hates that engine (though it did cost him a packet) and he begrudges it the professional care that could have kept it in good health.

A new attempt by Louis results in a desolate string of half-hearted, hollow bursts. The skipper has had enough, all the more so because onlookers on the pier and on the tug are giving exasperating advice. 'Drop the whole thing. We'll hoist it by hand.'

There are eight of us now, straining on the two halyards that hoist both ends of the gaff (peak and mast). Each of our efforts gains barely ten inches of halyard. The wail of a block at the masthead answers our breathing, while, with infinite slowness, the main-sail majestically rises and unfurls.

Fully spread at last, it hangs nearly motionless. Now and then, a waft of the faint breeze of dawn, further deflected by the quay, causes the weatherbeaten red cloth to shiver and flap with a sudden noise.

The effort has been exhausting. The skipper calls to the boy, 'Bring up the bottle of red,' and, after a brief hesitation (for he is close-fisted), 'and also white, for those who prefer it.' It must be said that every man receives two litres of red wine a day. Apart from this daily ration, which everyone is free to drink when he chooses, some circumstances call for a collective, cer-emonial drink – for instance, any heavy manoeuvre that requires everyone's participation. If the effort has been particularly demanding, the special occasion is marked by a choice between red and white.

The boy brings the bottles and the glass because, while everyone has his own mug for ordinary use, this wine ritual is performed with the boat's one and only glass. The boy fills the glass to the brim and presents it to the skipper, whose privilege it is to drink first. The glass is emptied in one gulp and given back to the boy, who fills it for old Félix. After Félix, there is no estab-lished order.

The jib is swiftly hoisted by two men. The tug passes us a tow; we cast off our mooring lines. In the past, there was no tug, and the sailing boats had to get in and out of port without assistance. But the skipper does not have enough trust in his crew to risk precise and fast tacking through a narrow pass which, moreover, is partly obstructed by a dangerous bar – a moving sandbank on which the sea breaks even at high tide.

The tug casts us off after we have crossed the bar. 'Free at sea by the grace of the wind,' *Prosper* heels gently, sniffs the wave and starts on her way. The rhythmic splash of the wave under her bows only deepens the wonderful silence that is the privilege of travelling under sail. In fine weather, with a steady breeze on her beam, *Prosper* is triumphant. She has all her sails up – we have set the staysail, the topsail and the jigger – and with her lee-rail close to the water, her long, slim stern is trailed by a turbulent and foaming wake. Poised on the shoulder of a regular, long swell, she points her bowsprit towards the pale blue horizon.

The boy starts to prepare a meal. He cooks on a coal stove secured in the sail hold. In this dark cavern, where powerful smells mix – tar, hemp, engine fumes, old cabbage soup, coal smoke – he gets the stove red-hot right next to the sails, the coils of rope and the petrol jerry-can for the windlass. When the sea is heavy, the stove is not used – the boy would not be able to hold the pot securely without getting burnt, nor to bring it up while the deck is being swept by waves. In such circumstances, he cooks in the corner of the quarters on a small gas stove. But when the boat heels beyond a certain angle, the flame, instead of heating the cooking pot, licks the bulkhead, which starts to burn – till someone notices it. 'Oh shit! It's burning!' And if a thrown gumboot does not stop it, a pot of cold water will, releasing a cloud of steam.

The boy is thirteen. This is his first fishing trip. To him, the men are what the sea is to them: a power of vast indifference that can be placated only by patience and shrewdness. The boy is therefore shifty, lazy and scrounging – this is how he survives in a tough world. It's not that the men are mean to him – for instance, when he peels the daily heap of potatoes, someone always gets out his knife and does half of the job – but rather, it's the way things are, a law that binds everyone, and nobody thinks to ease it for him because of his tender years.

His main job is to cook. This does not require any special skill, it is enough to toss potatoes, onions, carrots, turnips and a piece of beef or pig's trotters into the huge cooking pot and let it all simmer till the men's appetite calls for it. The only variation is that, once fishing begins, tuna will replace meat. The skipper buys just enough meat to last till the first fish is caught. From then on, for the next month, tuna – boiled, fried or raw with vinegar – will be the basis of all noon and evening meals.

It is also the boy's duty to attend to the small comforts of life on board: the morning coffee, the evening tea, the (relative) cleanliness of the quarters. He is supposed to find, and bring to whomever calls for it, marlinspike and twine, or tobacco and lighter. As far as he is able, he helps in all manoeuvres, without being told twice. In fact, he is told nothing at all: he must keep his eyes open and guess.

For the first few days, he is seasick. Nobody pays him any attention, no matter how green he turns, so long as he does his work. Grinding his teeth, he keeps an eye on the cooking pot in the smelly hold. From time to time, he comes up to vomit leeward, then goes down again. His seasickness will disappear – his childhood too. He will return a small thirteen-year-old grown-up, without dreams or games.

*

By late afternoon, the wind has abated completely; we are becalmed abeam of Groix. The sea is sluggish, the sails hang; *Prosper* rocks slowly on an invisible and lazy swell.

Old Félix is on watch. He sits comfortably, leaning on the tiller, which is useless for the time being, as the boat isn't moving. Crouching, compact, weather-beaten, he seems asleep, but his sharp little eyes are fully alive, scrutinising the horizon, inspecting the rigging, checking the compass. A man of his experience – he is sixty-two, with fifty years at sea – knows that even in fair weather one never relaxes one's vigilance. 'Yes, my boy, I am just an old cunt ...' Most of his remarks begin this way, but what he says is respectfully listened to by all. And when the weather turns foul, the skipper himself always asks for his opinion. In the handling of the boat, he may be slower than the others, but he uses his strength sparingly, to maximum effect; and when the wind, the sea and the boat demand it, he forgets his age and wholeheartedly throws himself into action.

Ten years ago he had throat cancer. The doctors gave him three weeks to live, but they operated on him nevertheless. Six months later he was still alive and, getting bored, decided to go back to sea. He has a big scar and practically no voice: just a hoarse whisper. This frustrates him when, during a difficult manoeuvre, he wants to shout abuse at a clumsy crewman and can manage only a sort of mute howl.

But in the evening, in the quarters after finishing his litre of wine, he talks. Since he can only use his voice sparingly, he has worked out a peculiar form of pungent and pithy maxim that endows even personal reminiscences with a sort of universal quality. There is, for instance, the story of his cancer, which everyone knows, having heard it so many times already. Even so, it is always listened to with pleasure, because it is such a stylish performance. Another favourite topic is his pet hatreds. He pursues four kinds of villains with the passion of one waging a religious war: 1. doctors; 2. Alain Bombard[†]; 3. scientists who send rockets to the moon; 4. the crews of cargo-boats.

Doctors, because they sentenced him to death ten years ago.

Bombard excites the collective hostility of many seamen for complex reasons. Firstly, because no skilled professional will ever accept that an amateur can teach him something essential about his craft. How can a

---

[†]   On the subject of Bombard, see page 22.

landlubber enlighten sailors on the basics of survival at sea? Secondly, Bombard upsets too many ingrained habits – such as to die when shipwrecked – and promotes new (and expensive) regulations – such as carrying life-saving equipment that actually works. Most fishing vessels carry 'life-boats' that could never be used in case of a shipwreck. *Prosper,* for instance, has only a ridiculous little dinghy, completely rotten, which could take no more than a third of the crew if it did not sink when put to water. As far as the fishermen are concerned, a life-boat has only two uses: to fulfil an administrative requirement of the Authorities; and to provide a convenient place to dump and store gear – sacks of coal, rope-coils, sail-cloth, baskets and crates. The life-rafts that Bombard wants to make compulsory, however, cost money and can only be used for their original purpose. The rest of the time, they must be kept carefully packed.[†]

[†] Such was the situation in 1958. Meanwhile the reforms advocated by Dr Bombard have been so universally adopted that nowadays most seamen are not even aware they were originally due to him. Only one criticism voiced by fishermen is still valid: Bombard effected his daring survival experiment in the tropical regions of the Atlantic – it could not have been done in colder waters. (Hypothermia kills more quickly than drowning.)

Scientists who send rockets to the moon are responsible for bad weather and rotten summers which harm fishing.

The crews of cargo-boats attract a mixture of hostility and contempt from the fishermen, especially from those who work under sail. Contempt because their lives are comfortable, and because they no longer know what seamanship is: they chip some rust here, daub some paint there ... Hostility, because each year collisions occur: fishing boats hove-to for the night are run down by cargo-boats because the men on watch, trusting their electronic equipment, have forgotten how to use their eyes.[†]

*

The wind has come up during the night. From her slumbering drift, *Prosper* wakes up with the first whiff of breeze. On my pallet, half-asleep, I hear the eerie whisper of the water running along the hull.

Towards dawn, the breeze freshens, the sea gets rougher. We are close-hauled, with reduced sail. *Prosper* makes lively attempts to head into the wind; she runs over the crests, confronts the waves with a deep

---

[†] In the meantime, technical progress has only made matters worse.

shuddering of all her ribs, while the spray jets up on both sides of her bows, in two geysers which fall, with a hissing sound, on deck. The helmsman strains to control and direct this new strength, like a rider reining in a fiery and clever horse. But *Prosper* seems to know by instinct how to meet the waves that attack her nearly head-on. The wind combs the tall crests into wisps of spray, but the boat avoids the heavier seas, easing sideways. While on top of a wave, we can see before us for a brief instant a wide expanse of sea-hills in long parallel lines, swelling up and collapsing, and then we dive into a new trough while the wave we just climbed flees under our stern …

Down below one hears another tune! Every wooden limb of the framework moans and creaks in the dark, and heavy, dull blows resonate through this hollow shell.

With such wind, we are moving fast. If it stays like this, we should reach the fishing grounds by tomorrow or the day after.

We are about to enter one of the most crowded and dangerous sea-lanes of the world, and we must cross it diagonally. Ships coming down from the Channel and the North Sea towards the Atlantic, the Mediterranean and the East, as well as all the return traffic, must squeeze through this passage. By the afternoon we can already see several silhouettes on the horizon. By evening, more ships appear, of all shapes and sizes, from small tramps to large tankers, with merchantmen and passenger boats of all nationalities. During the day, *Prosper* is quite visible with her tall red sail, but to signal her presence at night she has only one tiny oil-burning storm-lamp hoisted at masthead. Such a pathetic little light is not likely to make much of an impression on the big ships that speed through the night without changing course by even one degree. When one of them gets too close, we must take evasive action. Although the laws of the sea give absolute right of way to all sailing craft, however small, over all motor vessels, however large, we cannot expect these monsters to take notice of us, especially at night; they would sink us and go on their way without even realising they'd had a collision.

Tonight the skipper will not get much sleep. He stays on deck, near the helmsman, and old Félix has joined them too. Down below the others sleep with one eye open, ready to jump on deck at first call.

The starless night is dark and cold. The breeze is fresh, but still manageable. Sea and sky form one massive blackness, punctuated by the navigation lights of ships. Some of these are going away, their distant lights twinkling and disappearing; some grow dangerously close.

A big liner, brightly lit, passes us one or two cable-lengths ahead; we had to change course to get out of her way. 'Ow! They are guzzling champagne but cannot see what's in front of them!' grumbles Etienne, who has the helm and puts *Prosper* back on course. Our wooden boat, which one long wave can carry, is a mere cork in the wake of that ship, which crushes three dozen such waves under her uncaring steel plates. How many hundreds of men does she carry? Up there, people laugh, play, dream, eat and sleep ... while we, a few feet above the water, surrounded by dancing lights, keep watch till dawn.

The next morning we see one or two more ships whose course is west of the main shipping lane, and then it is over, we are through the dangerous passage and we find ourselves alone on the empty sea – at home.

On deck, only the helmsman is needed on watch. Down below, we chat. Oh, the endless talk in the quarters! First, there are various comments on the local news in *La Liberté du Morbihan*, of which we carry all of last month's issues. When these literary sources have run dry, we fall back on oral traditions: our collection of incidents, anecdotes and jokes is well-worn, but still serviceable. One draws from it sparingly: a good story can last as long as a pair of clogs. And some topics are inexhaustible: for instance, whether someone's wife is unfaithful, or was, or shall be …

Occasionally the skipper recounts some of the experiences of his youth. He is not uneducated, he has travelled. At twenty, he gave up fishing to join the Navy, where he had a full career. Having visited a few sailors' dens in the Far East, he enjoys the prestige of a man of the world, and his exotic tales still beguile his listeners.

When pensioned off as chief petty officer, he returned with his wife and two grown-up children to the little harbour where he was born. He could have lived there quite comfortably: besides his pension, his wife is well-off and he has two or three houses which he lets to vacationers. But he became bored and so bought *Prosper* and went back to sea. He does not need the income and, anyhow, the boat does not earn much once one has considered the cost of running and maintaining it. Every year, therefore, he says that this will be his last season, but when the season ends he postpones the date of his retirement and prepares *Prosper* for another run. On shore, he wilts and feels the weight of his age. At the helm of his boat, he reclaims the strength of his youth.

On such a sailing boat, the skipper is very close to his crew. They call him Maurice, and he works as hard as they do, keeping watch at the helm and lending a hand in all the heavy manoeuvres; whereas, on the *pinasses*, the skipper merely supervises from the bridge. As a result, the crew respects Maurice all the more. Besides, he is the only one on board who understands theoretical and astronomical navigation and can calculate the boat's position, though he practically never uses the sextant: his navigation by dead-reckoning is amazingly accurate.[†]

His power is absolute, and he takes full responsibility for it. When things are difficult, he takes the helm and only his voice can be heard; the others are silent and carry out his orders without question.

He may have cast off his uniform to wear once more the old beret and clogs of a Breton fisherman, but he has kept the discipline and customs of the Navy. He still follows practices that recall the dignity of his former

---

[†]   Needless to say all the electronic equipment which today is on even modest yachts, did not exist at the time, and *Prosper* had no electricity, batteries or generator.

rank – for instance, he addresses everyone as 'vous'[†], while all the others use 'tu'. Or one day, just as the boy had just brought up the midday meal – it was time for it – he said coldly: 'I have not said to bring the soup.' The boy had to carry the huge heavy pot all the way back to the stove in the for'ard hold – it was not easy, there was a heavy swell – and as soon as he had done this, the skipper said: 'Tell François to bring the soup.'

Maurice is always smiling, but deep down he is cold and hard. He has remarkable self-control, and an intuitive grasp of the psychology of leadership that gives him great authority over his men. I remember an incident with Robert as we were unloading the fish in port. With the splendid prodigality of a drunk, Robert wanted to throw a big tuna, just out of the hold, to some tourists who had hailed him from the quay. Maurice took the tuna from Robert's hands. Robert's euphoria at once became black rage: '*Nom de Dieu!* You did not catch them all by yourself! And if I want to give one to somebody?' And he continued with a long diatribe, a mixture of insults and old grudges. Suddenly he stopped. Maurice had not moved, just stared at Robert

---

[†]   In conversation, of course. As for all the nautical commands, as a rule, they are always expressed in the second person singular.

with icy calm. A long silence followed. Then the skipper said in a neutral tone, without raising his voice: 'Go away.' And Robert went away, sheepishly, like a schoolboy, and came back only when sober. The incident was over, and was not mentioned again.

In any case, Maurice would have been very annoyed to lose Robert, who is the youngest and the strongest of the crew, and, after Félix, the best sailor. And Robert would have been even more distressed had he quarrelled with the skipper and thus not been able to sail again with *Prosper*. He had already declined several offers – and better-paid ones, too – from skippers of *pinasses* because he wants to keep sailing with his uncle Félix, whom he loves and worships. In handling the boat, whenever a special effort is needed, he always manages to stand near Félix and uses his great strength to ease the old man's work.

Robert is built like a gorilla, but has as much heart as brawn. One pleasure that he cannot resist, however, is to drive Gabi mad. Gabi is the only victim he can needle at leisure. Since Robert stutters, he cannot attack foes who have a quick tongue. But Gabi is a true Breton; he barely speaks French (he uses it mostly in songs, but there, curiously, his traditional repertoire is quite wide) and therefore he is always slow to respond. In some ways, Gabi is the butt of everyone; he looks like a farmer who has become a sailor by mistake, and is easily mocked. He is not really clumsy, but he is a bit slow and cannot perform a task without Robert hurling abuse: 'Sailor-like-my-sister! Battlement lobster! One-armed fool! Country pharmacist!' These insults leave Gabi unmoved. Incapable of participating in the conversations in the quarters, he leads a rather withdrawn life. Well-settled in his bunk, he sips his wine with keen enjoyment, or cuts himself a slice of sausage carefully selected from the little collection in his basket. At night when he is at the helm, he sings long, old ballads to himself, first with a low voice, because he doesn't want the others to laugh. But once they are asleep, his voice gains in strength:

> *I have two big oxen in my shed.*
> *Two big white oxen …*†

*

---

† The song must be old. Flaubert alludes to it in *L'Education sentimentale*, part II, chapter VI, when there is a small party at Dussardier's to celebrate the liberation of Sénécal. Then, the pharmacist starts to sing it while preparing the punch. Gabi's version included a sentiment along the lines of, 'I'd rather see my wife perish instead of my oxen,' but I do not remember the exact words.

We are nearing the fishing grounds. The skipper prepares the fishing hooks himself, putting on each a lure made from a tuft of coloured horsehair – some red, some white, some yellow. The men rig the lines on the two booms. Once the hooks are tied on the lines, the booms are lowered to sit above the water, one on each side of the boat. Longer than the mast is tall, they spread like the two scraggy wings of a gigantic bird. The boat sails on, fishing has begun. The principle is simple: each boom trails seven lines, whose parallel threads are near the surface. These fourteen lines comb the sea with their light network. Now all we need to do is wait until the tuna decide to bite. The helmsman keeps a constant watch. The layman sees only fourteen lines equally stretched by the speed and the water drag, but as soon as a tuna swallows a hook the tautening of the line is as obvious to any fisherman as it is invisible to me.

[2005 postscript] After the original publication of this book, I received various letters from readers who knew the song and communicated the complete text to me. 'Les Boeufs' was written by the proletarian poet Pierre Dupont, and it figures in the 1851 edition of his collected *Chants et chansons*. (This volume was graced with a Preface by Charles Baudelaire.) My memory did not deceive me: the refrain of the song is indeed:

J'aime Jeanne ma femme, eh bien! j'aimerais mieux
La voir mourir, que voir mourir mes boeufs.

One can wait for days without catching anything. Boats can take a month to bring back a paltry catch. On the other hand, sometimes five or six lucky days are enough to fill the fish hold. Sometimes the tuna are caught by the dozen; non-stop, they stupidly rush after the lures which, because of their speed in the water, seem alive. But sometimes the lures do not work. It may be because the boat is too slow, or too fast, or the lines are too old, or too new – not to mention all the other imponderables like the time of the day, weather, state of the sea, water temperature … In the same spot, one boat may be catching endlessly while another drags her hooks without success. The most experienced fishermen have not yet finished exploring the mysteries of tuna fishing. The old tricks of the trade are closer to superstitious rituals than rational methods; and if one asks why do this or that, the answer is always the same: 'It is more *pêchant*' ('better-fishing'). Sometimes a whole boat is given such a description, and this final judgment (or its opposite) when pronounced by an expert is enough to bring confidence – or to call down a curse.

In the days before the use of ice, fishing was even more at the mercy of chance. Catching the fish was not enough; one had to preserve it until home was reached. Tuna were heaped on deck, under tarpaulins, but a sudden change in the weather was enough for bad luck to strike and cause the whole catch to rot at once. A few days from port, one had then to throw away the results of a month's work.

Because tuna are reputed to be temperamental and suspicious, tuna fishing is governed by many strict traditions. For a long time, it was done exclusively in sailing boats. The fishermen were convinced that iron hulls, engine noise and the water turbulence created by the screws would scare the fish away. Eventually some modern ship-owners looking for new profits risked the construction of motor boats for tuna fishing. Experience soon showed that the new *pinasses*, despite the cost of fuel, brought better returns. Thanks to their engines, they could move faster and, above all, once the fishing was completed, they did not have to depend on the wind's vagaries to return home and sell their catch.

Therefore, sailing boats vanished. They have now completely disappeared. (In 1958, out of the vast fleet that the French sent to fish for tuna, from Concarneau to St Jean de Luz, no more than half a dozen boats were still working under sail.)

*

'Third line on port!' yells the helmsman. Etienne and Louis jump on deck. The first catch of this *marée*! Louis hauls on the bracing wire and starts to wind up the line. Bent over the rail, Etienne waits for the moment when the catch will be alongside the boat. He grasps the *bazh-kroch* (boat-hook)[†], a long gaff at the end of which is an iron hook; it is used to lift the fish out of the water. Etienne eases the line that might otherwise snap under the weight of the catch.

At last, we see at the end of the line a white form writhing in the water. Etienne hooks it with the *bazh-kroch* and brings on board a superb fish, its tail slapping noisily on the planking. 'Ah, the swine! A blue!' Yes, it is a blue shark. Etienne secures it under his boot, pulls out the hook; with a slash of his knife, he nearly decapitates the shark, which shudders in frenzy, and then he throws the creature overboard. A bloodstain remains, evidence of an unwanted guest.

By the end of the day, five or six tuna have bitten. After being brought on board with the *bazh-kroch*, they still struggle fiercely and must be killed with a stab to a

---

[†]   They always called it by its Breton name, which, in the original edition of my book, I misspelled phonetically as 'basse-croque'. A reader from Brittany corrected me (*bazh* means 'stick', and *kroch*, 'hook').

precise spot on the head. They are cleaned, rinsed and placed in the ice of the hold, except one, which the boy hangs by the tail on the jigger-mast to be eaten at future meals. Every day slices will be cut from it, as from a huge loaf of bread.

Fishing days. The sea wipes away time. In the week, only two reference points remain, Sundays and Thursdays, because on these days, in addition to the wine, the skipper orders bottles of aperitif to be opened.

Luck is uneven. Sometimes the hours sink in the void, but sometimes one ends the day with a broken back from stretching the *bazh-kroch* over the rail to hook one tuna after another. At night, the boat is hove-to, and the man on watch can spend most of the time down below; he only needs to thrust his head out now and then to check that the masthead light is burning bright, while *Prosper*, left to herself, drifts slowly.

One afternoon, the wind begins to freshen. We've had a few squalls before, but this is more serious. The troughs deepen, the crests grow white. We have already hauled down the staysail and the jigger. Now we must replace the jib with a storm jib and bring the mainsail down to the third reef. The lines have already been brought in, and the booms secured. For these manoeuvres, the skipper takes the helm. All the men are at the halyards, hurrying and stumbling in their boots on the slippery deck. The wet ropes jam, the canvas stiffened by the wind cannot be smothered, green seas hit the deck and the men at work are drenched with icy spray. Suddenly the whole boat shudders and rolls as the helmsman lets her come into the wind so the men can tauten the halyards.

Once the storm sails are set, the men go down below. Under reduced sail, *Prosper* has found her new balance despite the fury of wind and sea, but the helmsman has had to rig a block and line on the tiller, and strains on it to keep control of the boat.

The sun sets with a yellow gleam under dark, low clouds and soon night comes, blotting out everything.

In the middle of the night we hear a tremendous crash in the rigging. The men on watch call out, while the boat rolls wildly. The crew is on deck immediately, half-clothed and barely awake. The mainsail is torn; wisps of canvas flap in the wind, while the peak, not restrained by the sail, swings high on the mast with savage jolts, causing the boat to lurch alarmingly.

In the black night, we have to haul down what remains of the sail and, most importantly, to restrain and secure the peak, which is sweeping everything from one side to the other. This is a difficult and dangerous manoeuvre. Afterwards there is nothing more to do except fasten everything on deck and rig a small mizzen sail. Thus, and with the helm lashed, *Prosper* can drift like a cork on the Atlantic swell, offering little resistance to the rush of wind and waves.

The grey dawn finds us in the same situation. The wind is stronger and whistles in the rigging; the mast stands oddly bare under a dull sky. With just a tiny bit of canvas for'ard and another aft, *Prosper,* left to her own devices, maintains a consistent course four or five points off the wind.

The mainsail gone, the fishing interrupted, the persisting heavy weather – none of this dents the fatalism of the crew. When the accident woke them up, they swore a good deal at first, but that was the end of it. Afterwards, among themselves they do not even discuss what has happened.

In such a situation there is nothing to do except wait down below, crowded in a damp space that reeks of fish and tobacco. We spend two days like this, sleeping, munching dry food and smoking. On the third day the weather eases and we are able to hoist a spare mainsail and resume fishing.

*

One morning, Félix, sitting aft and cleaning a tuna, gets a nose-bleed. The others don't pay attention at first, but as he is still bleeding a quarter of an hour later, they begin to worry, especially his nephew, Robert.

They give him a towel for a handkerchief. After a while, Robert has to rinse it in a bucket of sea water and the water turns brown and cloudy. This has to be repeated several times, the old man holding the towel to his face, then rinsing and wringing it out.

Robert finally persuades Félix to go down below and lie on his bunk. 'But I am not sick!' he protests. By evening, the bleeding still has not stopped. Robert is consumed with anxiety. He stays near his uncle, trying to second-guess his wishes in order to spare him the effort of speaking. He leaves him only to wash the towel, by now a rag, or to make him some tea.

Under the hatch, using the last light of day, the skipper looks up the medical chapter in *L' Almanach du marin breton*. He has taken off his beret and put on glasses with iron frames. I look down on his bald skull from above, and I realise suddenly that he too is an old man.

L' Almanach du marin breton doesn't help us to diagnose or cure Félix's condition. Someone puts cottonwool in his nostrils; Robert opens a tin of condensed milk and feeds it to him with a spoon.

The skipper is in a bind. If Félix's problem is serious, we should set sail for home right away. Yet to abandon fishing, waste days going back to Etel ... and how many more days will it be before we can leave port and start fishing again?

The men are silent. Robert is mad with worry and wants to go back immediately. Finally the skipper says: 'Haul in the lines and ready to bear off.'

We gybe on a rather steep sea and head back to France. Meanwhile night has fallen. Despite the strong breeze, *Prosper* has nearly all her canvas up and is broad-running, powerfully shouldered by a long swell. She tears through the water, leaving behind her a white wake that foams and shines in the dark.

Robert watches over the old man the whole night. Whenever Félix wakes up, he gives him a few spoonfuls of condensed milk. Restless at first, Félix finally calms down; by dawn he is exhausted and very weak.

The next evening we glimpse the light of Belle-Ile, and around midnight we heave to athwart of Groix. By sunrise, we see the coast of Etel and the entrance of the port a few miles ahead of us. The men prepare for landing, the anchor is stowed and the chain is put in the hawse-hole. Then, filling their coffee mugs with water, they all shave. Once they are clean and shaved, the jib is sheeted to leeward and *Prosper* heads for shore.

But then the wind drops. The sun climbs in a blue sky, announcing a glorious summer day. Despite having all her sails up, including the topsail, *Prosper* is practically motionless on a sea that is as smooth as a mill-pond. A basket is hoisted to the masthead to tell the signal-station that a tug is required.

Félix is getting restless again. He wants a mirror. Anxiously he asks: 'What do I look like now? How is my face?'

*

Once *Prosper* is alongside the quay, news of the mishap spreads quickly. Robert and Etienne carry Félix to a taxi. His old wife is there, clad in black, her face hard and calm – all her anguish is in her eyes.

Some time later, Robert comes back to fetch his uncle's belongings.

Louis and I help him because there are several parcels: boots, a kit-bag, oilskins and a curious wooden box now black with age. On its lid are carved a compass, an anchor and other nautical symbols. Robert is already half-drunk. Only he is allowed to carry the box, nobody else should touch it, he says. Stuttering and crying, he tells me a long and obscure tale from which it emerges that Robert's father gave the box to Félix with instructions to pass it on eventually to Robert. Its contents remain shrouded in mystery: it seems it has something to do with the horn of an ox (?), but here Robert's explanations become very muddled indeed. Under the pretence of fetching a cart on the other side of town for Félix's belongings, Robert and Louis drag me to all the cafés. After each one, we realise we have forgotten something – a gumboot, a pack, even the precious box – and we have to go back, drink another glass, and move on to the next station, where keeping all the luggage together becomes even more of a problem. At long last, we arrive at Félix's place, where drinks are immediately poured to thank us for taking the trouble …

*

Félix's condition is serious, but stable. The doctor thinks that the nose-bleed might have saved him from a stroke. The skipper does not want to waste too much time ashore. To fill Félix's place, he has signed on someone called Job. Job is a former cargo-boat mechanic. *Prosper* will sail tomorrow morning with the first tide.

I cannot sail with her, because I must be in Marseilles next month: my passage to the Far East is already booked on the *Messageries Maritimes* liner.

I go with the tug to see off my friends. We shout our goodbyes when the towline is cast off. The skipper is at the helm. For'ard, Robert and Gabi are hoisting the staysail, and despite the distance one can hear a familiar voice: 'One-armed fool! Country pharmacist!' A fresh breeze is blowing. *Prosper* gracefully tilts her tall red sail and is soon lost to sight.

*

Three months later, I was in another world, living in a crowded dormitory and immersed in the brimming life of a Chinese university. One day I was astonished to find on our communal table a long letter that brought me, after much delay, the epilogue of the narrative you have just read.

As I have mentioned, I was not the only passenger on *Prosper*. There was another, a lad of my age, rather silent in a friendly way, a Breton in love with the sea. As a child, he had lost the use of one eye, and this prevented him from entering the *École navale*. He was champing at the bit, working as a junior master in a high school in Lorient, and, like me, could only sail during the holidays. The *marée* we had experienced together had made us close. After Félix's accident, he sailed again with *Prosper*. Before leaving Europe, I had written to ask him about this second trip. His answer was delayed in the post, and then forwarded by ordinary mail to my new Chinese address.

When I received it, I was already so far from the *Prosper* experience that the impact of this sudden evocation was for me all the more powerful. Here it is:

My second trip was as varied as the first, the one we did together. We had all kinds of weather, from dead calm to storm. But at all times Prosper *behaved well.*

You will recall our departure. There was a stiff breeze – so much so that the skipper hesitated about sailing on that day, all the more because it was a head wind. But Monsieur Pessel does not like to waste time …

At the end of the first week, we saw a sail on the horizon. It was a tuna-fishing boat from Groix. We caught up with her, and both skippers chatted. They decided to sail in company, but the weather upset these plans. One night of stormy weather drove us apart, and we did not see the Groisillon again that marée.

Over the next fortnight the weather was sometimes fair, sometimes heavy. Only during the last week did the conditions become ideal for fishing. But we didn't catch much: the marée *was mediocre. We brought back 300 tuna (big and half) and 50 bonitos. The* pinasses *didn't do much better, in fact – and for them this was a disaster.*

Upon our return, there was a tragedy. The day the fish were sold, Robert could not be found. It was only in the afternoon that his mother discovered him in the loft: he had hanged himself and was quite dead. What could have gone on in his head? Poor Robert! But he had been drunk from the moment we landed.

The crew was to lose yet another member: Etienne, who drowned during the Bombard demonstration. (As you must have seen in the papers, Bombard came here to demonstrate his new life-raft. The raft was to be towed to sea by the Etel life-boat in which Etienne was a volunteer crewman. The engine stalled and the boat capsized on the sandbar. I wasn't in Etel that day, so I cannot give more details – I just read it in the papers …)

The last time I saw the crew of Prosper *was at Etienne's funeral. Old Félix was there. He seems to have completely recovered, and plans to sail again next year. But it must be said that in Brittany, funerals are always the occasion for some euphoria, induced by libations to honour the dead …*

ACKNOWLEDGMENTS

To translate one's own work can be quite unsettling. My cousin Jean-Pierre Ryckmans had the patience and kindness (once again – for he did this thirty years ago for the American edition of *Chinese Shadows*) to prepare a close rendition of my original French. His draft liberated me from my 'translator's block' and I became free to adapt it into this final version which, in turn, Nadine Davidoff and Chris Feik prepared for publication with their customary tact and skill. Thus, both at the start and at the end of my enterprise, I was very fortunate indeed to benefit from such generous and talented help – which I wish to acknowledge here, with deep gratitude.

S.L